About the Author

Hailing from County Louth, Éanna Ní Lamhna is a self-styled expert on just about everything. She is best known for her environmental expertise as a broadcaster on both the television series *Creature Feature* and the radio programme *Mooney Goes Wild*. Her ability to bring her subject to life is legendary and her no-nonsense approach to romantic views about wildlife are well known. She is currently the president of An Taisce, The National Trust for Ireland

Originally a botanist, Éanna is now a jack-of-all-trades, lecturing in St Patrick's Teacher Training College and DIT, conducting Leaving Cert ecology trips and inspiring environmental awareness in primary schools. She is married with three children and lives in Dublin.

Her first book, *Talking Wild – Wildlife on the Radio*, was published by TownHouse in 2002.

D1584677

WILD AND
WONDERFUL

ÉANNA NÍ LAMHNA

TOWN
HOUSE
DUBLIN

First published in 2004 by

TownHouse, Dublin
THCH Ltd
Trinity House
Charleston Road
Ranelagh
Dublin 6
Ireland

www.townhouse.ie

1 2 3 4 5 6 7 8 9 10

ISBN: 1-86059-218-X

Printed by
Creative Print and Design (Wales), Ebbw Vale

CONTENTS

Acknowledgements   ix

1   A Culchie Abroad   1

2   Surrounded by Water   13

3   Why you Can't Burn Holes in the Ozone Layer from your Back Garden   19

4   Flying in the Red Sea   31

5   Hummingbirds: Real and Pretend   39

6   Talking Wild in Costa Rica   45

7   Designed to Kill   55

8   Beautiful Water Police   65

9   Slithery Things in the Rivers   77

10   How to Boil an Egg in a Sock   89

11   Things that Sparkle in the Night   99

12   Deconstructing the Tale of the Salmon of Knowledge   109

13	The Exciting Life of the Courtroom Scientist	119
14	Not Sailing to Australia	127
15	Sex, Drugs and Rock'n'Roll in the Dark Garden	135
16	The Ones that Got Away	149
17	Carnival of the Carnivores	155
18	She Finds Seashells on the Seashore	167
19	Timberrrrrr!	177
20	Mooney Goes Wild	185
21	The State of our Environment	193
22	Teaching Students – or *not* Teaching them	203
23	Having a Whale of a Time	209

For my good friends, Michael and Betty,
who showed me Africa

ACKNOWLEDGEMENTS

Do the people I mention in this book really wish to be acknowledged?

My thanks must go to the listeners and contributors to the radio programme, *Mooney Goes Wild*, who unwittingly contributed to this book. Thanks to Derek Mooney for enduring the ribbing and banter he receives from me on air.

Jervis Good regaled me with stories of being a biological scientist. Michael Dillon commiserated with me on my students and added a string of his own student anecdotes. Richard Collins was his usual kind, helpful self. My family long-sufferingly put up with being neglected and fobbed off with fast food as deadlines (for me) approached.

To one and all, thanks.

A CULCHIE ABROAD

WHEN I WAS GROWING UP in the 1950s I never thought I'd go abroad anywhere. Sure, we had relations in America, but that was like another planet. We wrote them letters and marvelled over the contents of the American parcels we received, but to go there ourselves was not something we dreamed of. And as for Africa! The name Timbuctoo conjured up an image of a place so strange that we couldn't even imagine it. But one thing we were sure of – the continent was crawling with ferocious animals and your life would be in danger just being there. Weren't there snakes and crocodiles and lions and tigers lurking round every corner? The people who lived there must be terribly brave and spend their lives in a state of constant alert. My

godmother, who lived in Uganda at that time, used to tell us when she'd come home about snakes in the shed and point out that you'd have to check your shoes every morning before putting them on, in case there was something nasty in them.

However, when I grew up and learnt a bit more about the world, Africa didn't seem such a terrible place. For a start, there are no tigers there – just lions; tigers are only found in Asia.

Ireland has a very small number of plant and animal species on a world scale – most of which are perfectly safe and harmless – so when I got the opportunity to go to Tanzania in 1990, I jumped at the chance. Tanzania is on the other side of the equator, on the eastern side of Africa, and much of the terrain is dominated by savannah grasslands. My friends Michael and Betty would take us on safari through this landscape and we would get to see much African wildlife.

We landed in Dar Es Salaam and drove straight to their house, which was in a village with lots of other houses, perhaps eight hours' drive away. I still remember how I felt when we arrived at the house. Walking up to the door from the Land Rover, I suddenly realised that I was in Africa and I began to feel apprehensive. Would I step on a poisonous snake? Would some dangerous flying insect bite me and give me a terrible disease (despite being injected to the gunwales with vaccinations for every disease known to man)? Were there monkeys in the trees, or would they be asleep now that it was dark? Never did a short walk from car to house seem so long. And nobody else was keeping a wary lookout at all, but they were all chatting nonchalantly as if it was perfectly safe – which, of course, it was. In order to see any wildlife of note we were going to have to go to the game reserves where people didn't live and where there was no cultivation of the land. Everywhere else was tilled, cultivated and densely inhabited. The chances of seeing a leopard or a warthog were zilch.

And indeed we did go on safari and we had to work hard to see what wildlife we did see. Animals are experts at camouflage, and it was really difficult to see things unless they moved. As we drove along, our host said 'Oh, look at the giraffes'. So we looked, but we could see nothing. African giraffes in the wild are huge – up to nineteen feet tall – but we couldn't see them, as they were the same colour as the grass they were grazing and the spots broke up their outline and shape. But when they moved we couldn't believe that we could have missed them.

Tanzania lies on and just south of the equator. We had learnt at school that the warmest place on the planet is all around the equator, so we packed very lightly and wondered how we would bear the terrible heat. What we didn't factor in, of course, was the other dictum we had learnt at school – the higher you go, the colder it gets. So when we reached the highlands towards the north of Tanzania in the early morning, it was very cold, so cold that the Masai people we met were all shrouded in warm

blankets. We, of course, were wearing our shorts and every single T-shirt we had brought and were still sporting skin of a fetching shade of blue. If we had only stopped to think, we would have realised that the top of the highest mountain in Africa, Kilimanjaro, though it is practically on the equator, is permanently snow-covered. I'll know to bring long trousers the next time.

The highlight of the whole trip was the time we spent in Ngorongoro game reserve. This is an area about seventeen miles in diameter, totally surrounded by the sides of a long-extinct volcano. It is now a huge grassland area with rivers and lakes. There is only one way in, down the side of the crater, and the animals that live here are confined to the area by the topography and are protected from interference. We were to camp here and see real wildlife first hand, so we pitched our tents close to some others and waited for dusk. Most movements of animals here are at dusk and dawn – it's too hot in the middle of the day, so these are the times to go out. Dusk falls quickly at six and dawn comes again twelve hours later – a long night for Irish people used to maybe only five hours of darkness in early July. Going out animal-watching in the dark is a mug's game: the animals can see much better in the dark than we can and can smell better and hear better and run faster. Wiser really to wait till dawn.

So we amused ourselves looking at the stars. It is quite true that the African sky is really, really full of stars. First of all there is no light pollution, and secondly it is a southern sky, so all the stars were completely unfamiliar to our eyes, which are used to Orion, the North Star and the Plough. We were working out which might be the Southern Cross when we were assailed by a bellow from an adjoining tent in an American accent asking us to stay quiet and go to bed. This at eight o'clock in the evening and us in Africa looking at the clearest and brightest sky we'd ever seen! Why do some people go abroad at all, we wondered, maybe a shade too loudly. Amazingly, they refused our invitation to come out and look through our binoculars at the stars.

Lying on the floor of the tent under a tarpaulin later on and shivering (we had never believed a sleeping-bag would be necessary in Africa) it struck me that only the width of the tent fabric separated us from the wild hordes of elephant, rhino, hippo and buffalo that roamed outside. They might well be merely herbivores, but if their grazing took them in the direction of our tent would we all be goners? But maybe they didn't graze at night. Did cows at home graze at night? Surely not! Just chattily as it were, I mentioned that grazing was a daytime activity, was it not? Our host (it was a big tent) replied that night was when the hippos left their water to graze on the surrounding banks, because it would be too hot for them during the day. And even at night they got panicky if they felt that they were too far away from the water and would suddenly turn and charge straight back to the water, flattening everything in their way in their panic. In fact, more people were killed by hippos every year than by any other large animal.

'And what will we do,' I asked faintly, 'if we hear hooves thundering in our direction?'

'Well,' came the reply, 'we have the panga.'

'What's that?' I asked, feeling that it must be some large-bore elephant-gun type of weapon.

He reached down and picked up a large, rusty-looking knife half the length of a sword. As you can imagine, I felt really safe then and slept deeply and peacefully all night in spite of the cold.

But of course our tent had not been pitched anywhere near the hippos or their water and so we were never actually in any danger. We were up long before dawn next day and out in the Land Rover to see what action there had been. The lionesses had made a kill and the male of the species was hoping to join them shortly for breakfast. I was amused to learn that the king of the beasts allows his womenfolk to find and kill food for him and then arrives calmly for breakfast. Evolution, how are you? It was a zebra that had been killed and when we arrived the lionesses had polished off the liver and the male was tearing at the carcass. A whole hierarchy of animals would in turn eat at the carcass. The hyenas were skulking near by, waiting for the lion to finish, and then it would be the turn of the jackals. Meanwhile, the vultures circled overhead, hoping for an opportunity to grab a quick bite. We drove away eventually, back for our own breakfast, and very nearly ran over a male lion the exact yellowish colour of the grass, who was sprawled out on the ground digesting his meal.

We swerved to avoid him and he looked at us disdainfully – the interlopers in his territory.

After a second night in our tents – and this time we star-watched at a safe distance from all other tents – we reluctantly returned to 'civilisation'. This took the form of a large tourist hotel just outside the crater. And after two days' camping, this appeared the height of luxury and bliss. But not so, it would seem, to everyone. At the service desk was a very irate American berating the manager. It turned out that the water supply to the hotel rooms was not constant. This being the dry season after all, water was not always available. It was not available when this particular American wanted to shower. He could not believe it. This was a top-class African hotel, he was paying top dollar and the water supply to his room was faulty. In that quiet, understated way that some Americans have, he demanded to speak to the president of Tanzania. It didn't take a feather out of the manager.

'No sir,' he said, 'you do not want to speak to the president. You need to talk to the plumber.'

Mind you, Americans in their own country can be quite dramatic as well. Instead of reading about deserts and their inhabitants and lecturing about them to my third-level biogeograpy students, I decided three years ago that the time had come to see some desert for myself. And where else to go but Death Valley in California, one of the hottest places on earth, day and night? We didn't go directly to Death Valley, but arrived first in San Francisco and then made our way eastwards, via Yosemite, where the biggest trees in the world – the giant redwoods – grow. It took several days to drive there and we interacted with the locals along the way. One surprising thing to me was the dominance of fast-food joints, to the exclusion of all else it seemed. In one place, despairing of ever eating anything again only pizza and burgers, I asked where was there a proper restaurant. The fast-food server looked at me in amazement. 'You mean, you want a sit-down meal? We only have sit-down meals at Thanksgiving and at Christmas.' He wasn't joking either.

Getting a drink with your pizza was another problem. This was California, where they grow grapes and make wine, for goodness' sake, but you were hardly in the door of any diner, when they were pouring out big jugs of minerals (which they called sodas), as if you had crashed a kids' party. But when you asked about wine it was *scéal eile*.

'What sort of wine do you want?'

'Well, what sort of wine do you have?'

'We have red and white.'

'Oh, OK. So we'll have red.'

And out came a quarter bottle to be shared between two of us. It wasn't bad, actually, so we summoned over the waitperson to get some more.

'More wine? Do you have a problem?'

The only problem we had with the drink was getting any.

Another interesting thing was how unfamiliar the

Americans were with the next place down the road. The next big tourist attraction after Yosemite is Death Valley. On leaving Yosemite, we asked at their advice desk about getting there, how long it would take, the best route, etc. If we had asked for guidance on the direct route to hell, we couldn't have been greeted with more horror. This was the month of July. We couldn't want to go to Death Valley. We wouldn't survive there. The temperature was 110. This last bit of information did fill us with alarm, until we realised that Americans use Fahrenheit, not Celsius, scales.

'Sure, aren't there towns in Death Valley? Don't people live there all the year round? How come they're not fried?' we asked.

Admittedly, the towns are called Furnace Creek and Stovepipe Wells, but even so. Of course, it transpired that none of the people we spoke to in Yosemite had ever been to Death Valley anyway. They recommended avoiding it altogether and going directly to Las Vegas, detouring back by Palm Springs, in case we melted going through Death Valley. This would only involve a detour of about five hundred miles. Naturally we ignored all such advice. We drove straight to Death Valley, where there were not only several towns but also a golf course open for business, which just goes to show that golfers are a breed apart the world over.

And what about the wildlife? Oh yeah, the wildlife. Well, in Yosemite we were warned under pain of all sorts of recriminations to leave no food anywhere, not even in the car, because it would attract the huge wild bears who inhabited the valley. But did we see a bear, or even a footprint? Did we ever. We were sorely tempted to scatter food about and wait in the car ourselves. We did, however, see the giant redwoods in a great stand of tall, soaring trunks. And truly no photos or television pictures can capture the majesty and presence of such trees. There is only a small number of stands left on the slopes of the Sierra Nevadas; the rest were felled for timber. Apparently they were so huge that when felled, the timber shattered on impact and was useful only for making matches. What an ignominious end for such mighty, long-lived trees!

We were nervous wrecks when we got to Death Valley. The car had a temperature display and it was rather off-putting to be getting readings of over one hundred at five o'clock in the morning, even if they were in Fahrenheit. The floor of the valley is below sea level, so the temperature rises as you descend into it. But we reached Zabriskie Point at sunrise and it was all worthwhile. The colours and shapes of the rock were fantastic in the true meaning of the word. The visitor centre and museum building is at Furnace Creek, where you can get your photo taken with the famous thermometer. Fifty-seven degrees Celsius or 134 Fahrenheit is the highest it has ever read (beaten only by a place in Libya). This reading was taken in July 1913. It only read a paltry 108 the July morning we were there – quite chilly really, by local standards.

We did go on to Las Vegas, which they were so

enthusiastically recommending in Yosemite, and believe it or not the temperature on the street there was 108 as well. Nobody was taking a blind bit of notice of it. It's only in Death Valley that you can die of the heat, apparently, not Las Vegas. Looking at Las Vegas, I could see why George Bush pooh-poohed any consideration of limiting greenhouse emissions. Not only Las Vegas in Nevada, but much of California as well, could not be lived in if it were not for the twenty-four-hour consumption of electricity to make the place habitable. And although the sun shines all the time, there seemed to be very little harnessing of it by way of solar panels. Why, for goodness' sake, when we washed our clothes while camping in Yosemite, we were requested to dry them in electric clothes dryers! It hadn't rained there for four years, but we were not permitted to hang out the clothes to dry. We draped them all over the car seats in an attempt to cool it down somewhat. They were dry in thirty minutes, even if the tone of the carpark was lowered by such wanton disobedience. We certainly saw no evidence of any awareness of the impact that the use of fossil fuels was having on the environment. Petrol was a quarter the price it is in Ireland. The car rental company nearly had apoplexy when they discovered that we intended to drive to Las Vegas in the car we were renting in San Francisco. It wasn't the fact that we were travelling that distance or taking a car here and leaving it there – no, it was the fact that the car was far too small for such a distance, we should upgrade ourselves by two stages. The car was perfectly

fine, but the attitude was, why have a small car when a big one was available and practically as cheap?

Mind you, that attitude seems to have reached Dublin now. The traffic-calming ramps and roadworks have surely not got to the stage yet where the four-wheel drives so abundantly encountered are actually necessary.

SURROUNDED BY WATER

MY FIRST DIVE EVER was in Coliemore Harbour in
Dalkey in Dublin Bay. A gang of nervous beginners, we
followed Rory Corvin down to thirty feet and sat on fish
boxes at the bottom of the harbour in a pale green light.
And we took a deep breath through our regulators, which
we had only ever used up to this in Tara Street baths. And lo
and behold, we could breathe. The equipment worked. We
could sit down there breathing and making ridiculous hand
signals at each other. I was so excited, I scarcely missed not
being able to talk. This dive marked the start of a few
exciting years with the Irish Sub-Aqua Club, when I got to
explore the Irish coastline underwater.

You could still dive in Dublin Bay in those days – the mid-

1970s. You could be forty foot down at the back of the Muglins on a summer's evening by seven o'clock, having completed a day's work in the city, travelled out to Coliemore Harbour and covered the rest of the distance to the back of Dalkey Island in an inflatable. There was such life to be seen down there. Dublin Bay was famous in Molly Malone's time for its mussels and they were still here in abundance in the 1970s. Mussels are filter feeders. They suck lots of water through their bodies and any food in that water they absorb. They cannot pick and choose what they will absorb – it all goes in. There was lots of food in Dublin Bay in those days: our waste treatment system had seen to that. Wasn't Dublin Bay big enough to dilute all the waste that the population of Dublin produced? Maybe, but what happened to the diluted waste? To be strictly scientific about it, this was food eaten by us, but not, of course, completely digested and absorbed by us. The diluted organic mixture was food for others in the food chain and filter feeders, like the mussels, loved it. They drew it through their bodies and thrived on it. There was a carpet of blue-black mussels on the bottom, right across Dalkey Sound from the shore, right to the Island and round the back to the Muglins. These mussels were food for the next lot in the food chain – the starfish.

Ordinary starfish have five tentacles with an eye at the end of each tentacle so that they can see whether they are coming or going. They grab hold of the mussels with these tentacles and prise them open. And then they extrude their stomachs out through their mouths, which are at the centre of their bodies on the underside. They poke their tummies into the opened mussels and envelop the tasty morsel, the living mussel body, inside. They then restore the stomach and the mussel flesh through their mouths, back down into their lower regions again. Wouldn't you just love to go out for a meal with a bunch of starfish! They don't confine their attentions to mussels, but will happily eat other bivalves too, such as scallops. One of our diving companions who was partial to the odd scallop used to wage war on the starfish. Not being fully *au fait* with the body structure of the creature, he used to cut it with his knife. But starfish being such primitive creatures, they could grow back new tentacles, so he was actually increasing the population by his activities rather than the other way round.

You'd want an iron constitution to eat the mussels of Dublin Bay in those days. As well as second-hand (or something) food, they also filter the bacterial contents of our waste into their bodies as well. And while a light boiling until the shells open may cook the mussel flesh, it doesn't kill bacteria. You'd need to boil them for thirteen minutes to be sure that all the bacteria are dead. What would your average mussel look like after being boiled for thirteen minutes? A tiny bit of yellow chewy rubber – that's what. The fever that Molly Malone died of was typhoid fever, probably contracted from eating the mussels she had for sale. People who were already suffering from typhoid at that time would have excreted the bacteria with their waste

into Dublin Bay, which would be absorbed by the filter-feeding mussels who lived there.

Or could the cockles have been to blame? These shellfish are also bivalves – that is they have two shells and they live buried in the mud in the very shallowest waters. When the tide is in and the mud is covered with water bearing lots of food, they stick up their filter, which is a long, tough white tube, and filter in the water. Any food in that water is theirs, and they expel the water again when they have absorbed it. So any baddies in the water – bacteria, poisons, heavy metals, whatever – will all be absorbed too. When the tide goes out, the mud flats lose their covering of water, so the cockles retreat down into the soft mud, pulling their feeding filter tube back into their shells. Walking over the mud at low tide, you can, with a practised eye, see the slight indentation they leave on the surface. Cockle-gatherers use rakes to comb the mud to dislodge the cockles, which do not bury themselves so very deep down. Cockle-gatherers have to work between the tides, often at night, and it can be a cold, thankless job. Many Irish people consider this type of food to be *bia bocht* – poor food eaten during famine times to ward off hunger – and have not much time for it now. It is much more popular in Britain and France than it is here.

The food chain is a wonderful thing. Diving in Dublin Bay in those days I was struck by the abundance and size of the crabs, particularly the edible crab. They were the size of dinner plates. I cod you not. And the wonderful thing about being a biologist diver was that you understood how the food chain worked. You couldn't risk eating the filter feeders, because the bacteria would get you. But you could eat whatever ate those, and crabs, and indeed lobsters, were at this level on the food chain. They ate the mussels, bacteria and all I suppose, but by absorbing this food into their own bodies they purified it. You could eat crabs with impunity out of Dublin Bay and lobsters too if you could find any. Crabs were given to walking along the bottom, feeding on the wall-to-wall mussels and you could select whichever one you wanted as you cruised slowly over them. Lobsters had the wit to hide in holes in the rocks and only emerge at night, so we didn't encounter too many of them at seven o'clock of a summer's evening.

Mind you, my greed was nearly the end of me one evening as I swam along selecting a crab for supper. I kept swapping the crab I was holding for an even bigger one, until eventually I was holding one as big as the dinner plate you'd be given in a fancy *nouvelle cuisine* restaurant. One holds a crab behind its front claws, as they cannot angle their claws back to get you. So, as I slowly finned back underwater, holding my crab up in my right hand, I began to notice that I could hardly draw any breath. Could I be out of air? No, the contents gauge reassuringly read quarter full. So why couldn't I breathe? Looking back at the air tube leading from my bottle to my breathing regulator, I saw to my horror that the crab had fastened one of its claws around the rubber tube and was closing in on it. And I had

greedily selected such a large crab that I couldn't prise the claw back open. Had I just drawn my last breath?

You never ever dive alone: I had a buddy. I got the chance at long last to use the Terrible Emergency Altogether signal – a hand drawn across your throat. And my buddy didn't panic. One twist of the trusty diving knife in the claw and the crab thought better of throttling me. It gave me great pleasure to cook it that night, even though it wouldn't fit in my largest pot and I had to bake it in the oven (having first of all dispatched it of course). I don't think I am cut out to be a vegetarian.

CHAPTER THREE

WHY YOU CAN'T BURN HOLES IN THE OZONE LAYER FROM YOUR BACK GARDEN

SPRING MOVES NORTH across Europe at the same speed as a person walks. The arrival of spring is heralded by the opening of the leaves on the trees, so that if you could look at Europe from the air you would see this green wave starting in southern Europe in February and moving north at about four miles an hour. It reaches Ireland in early April and if you take a European holiday at this time you will always be struck by how different things look at your destination. It will be much greener if you go south, while if you go to Denmark, say, spring has not yet arrived at all.

This has all been described recently from satellite images that are taken of our world from space. Climate scientists compare these images, one year against the next, and they have discovered that spring is starting its march earlier and earlier each year. Our climate is changing – rapidly – and we are all affected by it.

If there's one thing that seems to be utterly confused in people's minds, and indeed in the minds of some of those in authority, it is this whole concept of climate change and what is causing it. How many times have I been told that burning rubbish in your back garden will damage the ozone layer? It will do no such thing. It would want to be a bonfire eighteen kilometres high. Or, that all that rain was caused by a hole in the ozone layer, as if it were some sort of punctured umbrella. Or, indeed, that cows are affecting the ozone layer! The thing is that there are two completely different environmental problems here. We found out about both at the same time, and in some people's minds, they are inextricably mixed up.

Let not the readers of this book complain that I did not do everything in my power to address this confusion. Let us start with the ozone layer. This is a thin layer at the very outside of the atmosphere that surrounds the earth. It is about eighteen kilometres above the earth and up there it is very cold and the pressure is very low. The atmosphere anywhere around the world has about 20 per cent oxygen in it. Normally this oxygen is in the form of two oxygen atoms stuck together to form an oxygen molecule, which we call O_2. However, on the extreme rim of the atmosphere, where it is very cold and the pressure is very low, the oxygen atoms go round in gangs of three. We call this O_3, or ozone. The ozone molecule has a different shape from the normal O_2 molecule found everywhere else in the atmosphere, because in this case there are three atoms bound together rather than two. (Are you with me so far?)

This layer of ozone (O_3) is a wonderful shield around the world, because it protects us from the very harmful ultraviolet rays of the sun. These rays are full of energy and, if they struck our skin, would damage our cells and cause cancers. The ultraviolet rays can pass though normal-shaped oxygen molecules but not through the quare-shaped ozone ones. So by and large, the general population is protected from virulent skin cancers, as indeed are animals and crops, by the existence of the ozone layer. But, of course, we have discovered a way to damage this wonderful protective ozone. We didn't do it deliberately, we didn't even know we were doing it, but damage it we did. We invented a wonderful new gas called chlorofluoro-carbon (CFC). This is for all the world like a three-piece jigsaw. Chemists looked at all the elements in the periodic table and picked three that would completely bond with each other, leaving no sticking-out sides as it were. These three all joined together like three jigsaw pieces and there were no grooves or promontories that could connect to any other jigsaw piece, or, in other words, to any other element.

21

It was complete in itself – an inert gas – and would do no harm to anybody. It would not react with anything, or so the thinking went; it was just a neutral filler and could be made very cheaply.

So CFC filled bubblewrap; it was put into cans under pressure to act as aerosols; it was put into expanded polystyrene, which was used as insulation; it was put into fridges and air-conditioning systems as part of the cooling operation. We were delighted with all these useful things and used them liberally. What we didn't realise, what nobody realised, was there was one thing that would react with the chlorofluorocarbons and that was the ozone in the ozone layer. When the CFCs were released into the air, they were able to drift unchanged throughout the atmosphere because they reacted with nothing. However, when they got to the outer layers, the very edge of the atmosphere, they were able to react with the ozone. They broke up the gangs of three and turned them back into ordinary oxygen, O_2, which, you will remember, allows nasty, cancer-causing ultraviolet rays through. This happened fastest in the dark in extreme cold, and the darkest, coldest time and place was winter over the poles. So, at the beginning of spring every year, about March in the northern hemisphere and September in the southern hemisphere, the amount of ozone over the polar regions was greatly reduced – the so-called ozone hole.

And we didn't know anything about it. We continued on our merry way, spraying our backcombed beehives with hairspray as if there was no tomorrow. And there might not have been either, if the cold war between Russia and America hadn't ended. Now what was America to do with all their spy planes that had been keeping an eye on Russia? They deployed them on scientific work, collecting samples of the atmosphere from very high up. Only in the early 1980s did we discover the damage to the ozone layer. The cause was quickly determined, and at the Montreal Convention at the end of that decade, it was agreed to stop using CFCs. Other, non-dangerous substances could replace them, which they did.

But it isn't as simple as that. The CFCs are very long-lasting. They will be up there for at least another fifty years, attacking our ozone. Fridges are very long-lasting too. Lots of us still have ones that were manufactured in the 1980s. There are, of course, facilities for disposing of them safely, when they come to the end of their life or must be replaced by the latest colour and design. However, these facilities are not in the middle of bogs, or in quarries or in ditches. Fridges chucked into these places, as well as looking awful, are actively continuing the damage to the ozone layer, as the CFCs leak from them. And it is our grandchildren who will cop it.

But at least we know about CFCs, and we have done something about it. Global warming is a second, *completely separate* environmental situation. We are looking now at a different part of the sun's rays and a different component of the atmosphere. The sun shines down upon the earth. The heat is carried to us as infrared radiation, which enters the atmosphere, warms us up, bounces off the earth and is reflected back into outer space. It comes and it goes. It is just like when a ball hits a wall, the wall slows down the speed of the ball and reflects it back in the opposite direction. Similarly, the heat rays are slowed down when they hit the earth and are reflected back out again at a slower speed than when they came in. And this slowing down of the heat rays changes their wavelength. They are longer when they are going out than they were coming in.

There are certain components in the atmosphere that are very responsive to these wavelengths. They will let them in all right, but the longer, changed shape can't get out again through them, and so the heat is trapped. The gases in the atmosphere that do this (block the infrared radiation from bouncing back, away from the earth) are called 'greenhouse gases' and chief among them is carbon dioxide. If the atmosphere was all carbon dioxide, no heat would escape, and this planet would be far too hot to live on. If we had no carbon dioxide at all, on the other hand, all the heat would escape and it would be too cold for us. But, like baby bear's porridge, the amount of carbon dioxide we have is just right, and we can live here grand. Or so we thought until recently.

Compared to oxygen (nearly 20 per cent) and nitrogen (80 per cent), we have very little carbon dioxide in the atmosphere – just .035 per cent or 35 parts per million. But it was only 27 parts per million two hundred years ago, which means that it has increased by a third over that period, and it is still increasing. Where does this carbon dioxide come from? Well, in the first place, carbon dioxide is not what you would call air pollution, as such. Every one of us breathes it out when we exhale. Plants take it in to grow as they carry out photosynthesis, and give out oxygen. We, and indeed all animals, breathe in oxygen and give out carbon dioxide. Neat, when the thing is balanced.

Now, plant bodies are made up of carbon, and as long as they stay as plants, this carbon is stored in them. But if they are destroyed or rot away, the carbon is released into the atmosphere as carbon dioxide. The amounts of carbon dioxide in the atmosphere have not always remained the same. We know that hundreds of millions of years ago, in the carboniferous era, there was much more carbon dioxide in the air than there is now, and the world was a much warmer place. It was covered with lots of forests that grew very fast. Just as our bogs today are great stores of plants that lived in Ireland hundreds of years ago, but did not rot when they died, the plants that lived at this time, millions of years ago, did not rot away either. They were compressed under the earth's surface and, depending on conditions, they became coal, oil and natural gas – in other words, fossil fuels. And the carbon dioxide that they took in from the air as they grew remained trapped in them. So, slowly, over millions of years, the carbon dioxide levels in the atmosphere were reduced, and the climate changed very gradually. (No nodding off at the back there, now.)

But in the recent past, we have found all these fossils fuels and we are burning them for energy. Oil for transport, coal for electricity, gas for heating, or vice versa. We get the energy and we release the carbon dioxide back into the air. What took millions of years to collect and store as fossil fuels, causing gradual change to the earth's climate at the time, we are releasing back into the air in one fell swoop, as it were, in tens of years, rather than millions.

And then, carbon dioxide is not the only greenhouse gas. Methane is one too. Anything that once lived produces methane if it rots away without any oxygen. This includes the contents of cows' stomachs where the hard-to-digest grass is fermenting away. (Michael Viney once described this phenomenon in *The Irish Times* as farting cows, and had to put up with 'refeened' people correcting him on what they presumed to be a typing error for 'farming cows'. It wasn't.) Landfill sites full of newspapers, old vegetables, chicken carcasses, don't just lie there quietly under their cover of soil when they are full and sealed. If they ever had any organic material, the contents are all fermenting away and producing methane. Left unattended to, this can be an explosive risk as well as a source of greenhouse gas. And, size for size, methane is much more efficient at trapping heat than carbon dioxide.

What would take some of this extra carbon dioxide out of the atmosphere? Well, large, fast-growing plants like trees would. Where are the greatest amounts and the fastest-growing trees in the world? In the tropical rain-forests, that's where. And what are we doing to our tropical rainforests? (Don't all shout together, put your hands up!) *We are cutting them down*, that's what. Are we mad or something?

Is it any wonder that there is unprecedented climate change – and it may not be all global *warming* either. There is a possibility that the warm Gulf Stream off our coast may be redirected, if too much fresh water from melting icecaps enters it, and then we'd be goosed altogether – our Irish weather could end up like that of Labrador, with snow for six months of the year!

So, burning fossil fuels increases the amount of carbon dioxide in the atmosphere. Burning rubbish in your garden does not burn holes in the ozone layer, but it does cause air pollution. Anyone downwind of such a fire will have to breathe in the smoke and, depending on what you have been burning, there may be very nasty things indeed in the smoke. Anything with plastic in it gives off dioxins when burnt at the relatively low temperatures your back-garden bonfire-in-a-barrel would attain. Dioxins can cause cancer. Burning rubbish is against the law in built-up areas. Fine. But what about burning rubbish, plastics and all, in incinerators? They do this all over Europe, and they are not dropping like flies from cancer. There is even an incinerator in a main street in Vienna in Austria. The science is that, burned at very high temperatures – and we are talking here about eight hundred degrees centigrade – dioxins are destroyed. This is what happens in those countries that use incineration successfully as a means of getting rid of rubbish. But mention the possibility of having an incinerator in this country, and there is uproar. People who the week before were seeking my advice on how to get rid of foxes, wasps, badgers, ants, whatever, are now wanting me to come down to their part of the country to explain how the proposed incinerator will spoil the habitat for them. People who want and demand clean air for their children throng the parish hall in a 'No to the Incinerator' meeting and then one-third of them light up their cigarettes, when they finally get outside when the meeting is over. It is hard to take the protests of people seriously, when it is they who have created all this household rubbish and yet can't be bothered sorting it, recycling it, cutting down on it in the first place. In this country of only four million people, there should be no need for any incinerator. We should not be making enough rubbish to keep even one going. And it's not really the manufacturers' faults, you know. If we didn't buy their over-packaged, un-recyclable goods, they couldn't sell them, and they'd soon stop producing them. We should vote with our shopping baskets.

But of course we will do nothing but complain, until we are beaten into doing something. We all knew deep down that we didn't actually need all those plastic bags. However, in 2001 we used two billion of them – that's 500 plastic bags for every man, woman and child in the country. And our hedgerows were witness. But only bearded save-the-earthers in sandals carried shopping bags, or so the thinking went. At fifteen cents a bag, the plastic bag tax would have eliminated the national deficit in one year. Two billion by fifteen cents equals three hundred million euro. Noel Dempsey, the minister who introduced the plastic bag tax through thick and thin, would be assured of a place in the history books. Well, he has his place, not because our national coffers are bulging, but because of our totally improved hedgerows. Use of plastic bags dropped by 90 per cent in one year. People were seen juggling their messages in the air, instead of forking out for a plastic bag. Sales of embarrassing things, like toilet paper, dropped in small shops, and people didn't buy extras if they had forgotten their shopping bags. You could teach an old dog new tricks, but only if you used lots of stick and no carrot.

We all know we didn't learn this at school. Environmental education only began in 1971. But in the twenty-first century, this excuse is no longer good enough. We didn't have computers in school in the old days and we can still send emails and book foreign holidays as to the manner born. We used to have to go down the road to the phone box, to receive calls from Dublin, which came via several operators along the way and got through accompanied by a terrible racket as button A released all the money the caller fed into the box (if you were lucky!). Now we can send pictures to Australia from our mobile phones. We

have no difficulty learning all these new technologies. We can do it right well if we want to. Sorting waste as you go, into different containers, isn't rocket science. Why don't we want to do it?

FLYING IN THE RED SEA

SCUBA DIVING is the nearest I'll ever get to flying. Really flying that is, like birds. When you want to go up, you kick your legs and up you go. When you want to go down, just put down your head and follow it. Correctly weighted, you are weightless under the sea and enjoy the same freedom that fish do. You can swim along over a rocky bottom and then, when you come to the edge of it, soar over the cliff down into the deeper water below. You can pause as you go down to examine the edge of the cliff and then stop going down and come back up when you want to. Just moving about in this weightless world is thrilling. When you factor in encounters with the denizens of the deep, the adrenalin rush can be mighty.

Plant life – large plant life that is – is surprisingly scarce under the sea. Seaweeds need light to grow. Not just any old light, but light with the correct wavelengths. Green plants, which contain chlorophyll, look green because they reflect green light. Seaweeds all have chlorophyll too, although they do not all look green. Brown and red seaweeds have other colour pigments as well, which give them different colours to our eyes, but it is the chlorophyll in them that enables them to do the business – the growing.

The wavelengths of light needed for growing cannot penetrate water very far, just down about ten metres in our not-so-transparent Irish waters, so all the growth in the sea by large seaweeds off our coasts takes place in the top ten-metre layer. The suspended algal plankton extends down somewhat further than this. Go down deeper than that in the sea, and you leave behind the world of plants. In fact, seeing seaweed is a sign that you have reached shallower water and is often a most welcome sight to a diver who has got a little lost.

Below ten metres or so, you also leave behind the world of colour as we are used to it. Although light may extend down to fifty metres or more, depending on the clarity of the water, all the rays of the spectrum won't, and so you see things down there in a sort of monochrome. Further down still, of course, are regions where light never penetrates – regions of perpetual darkness – but they are below the zones of sports diving so I can't report from there.

The furthest down I have ever been was to fifty metres and that was in the Red Sea in the Gulf of Aqaba. Here there is a great cliff going straight down to over three hundred metres just in off the edge of the sea. You trudge in off the shore in about forty degrees of heat in your thick, seven-millimetre rubber wetsuit designed for Irish weather, to the sneers of the affluent Germans in their three-millimetre suits: 'You must be such cold persons to need such thick suits.' But our skins are as thick as the suits and we ignore such comments. We have the wonders of the world to see and our thick suits will protect us from any nasty coral scrapes or over-enthusiastic fish! Ten steps in the water and we are at the cliff edge and down you go – carefully, carefully, keeping an eye on the depth gauge. The deeper you go, the shorter the dive, so if you go for the fifty metres, you'll only have about five minutes there. The pressure is about six times that at the surface, and the air in your bottle won't last long at that depth.

It's still bright down here, but it is not silent. You can hear every breath you draw shrieking through your air regulator. Is it really built for this depth? you wonder. If ever you depended on equipment, you're depending on it now. You can hear banging noises in the water and realise that it is pile-driving going on in Aqaba on the other side of the Red Sea, say fifty miles away. You can't hear that at all above. So it's true what the physics books say, sound travels better in liquids than in air. Bet the Native Americans could hear the trains miles away by putting their ears to the tracks and

it wasn't just a figment of the *Beano* and *Dandy* illustrators' imaginations.

But I didn't come down here to think about the *Dandy*. What lives here? Well, sharks do, actually. Nurse reef sharks. These are large sharks that cruise just off the rock faces and, yes, I can see two swimming in a semi-circle around me as I gaze out with my back to the cliff. It says in the books that these are harmless and only attack injured fish. I hope that they have read the same books, that my swimming technique is better than that of an injured fish and that I am not sending out the wrong signals. Far, far below I can just make out other sharks with peculiar-looking heads. These are hammerhead sharks, so called because their heads look like the top of a lump hammer with an eye at the edge of each 'hammer face'. God only knows where their mouth is – hope I'm not about to find out. These sharks can be dangerous enough, but these particular ones are staying far below.

All the while, I am breathing normal air out of my bottle – 20 per cent oxygen and 80 per cent nitrogen, just like we all do every day. But down here the whole shebang is at six atmospheres of pressure, me and the air in the bottle. Nitrogen at this pressure in the blood can give rise to a condition called the narcs (which is quite different to the more notorious bends). Having the narcs is like being drunk – if I get up off this bar stool, I'll fall over – or, as it is known in the posher diving books, 'the Martini effect'. Divers are warned to be on the lookout for it in themselves and in each other. You don't know until you are down at this great depth whether you'll suffer from it or not, but look out for any odd symptoms. I knew I was getting the narcs when I saw, just in front of my mask, the weirdest-looking fish. It appeared to be bright green as I shone my torch on it, and it seemed to be very short and high, instead of long and slender and streamlined like fish are. This one looked as if someone had adjusted the vertical button too much and stretched it in the wrong direction. But what confirmed my suspicions was the fact that this fish had an enormous bump on the top of its head as if it had been hit over the head with a stick. Definitely time to move up, as the narcs wears off immediately you ascend and doesn't leave you with a hangover.

Moving up from such depths takes ages, because, as you come up, the pressure gets less. The effect is the same as releasing the lid on a bottle of soda water. Do it suddenly, and the carbon will fizz out of the water and cause it to overflow. Come up too quickly, and the air in your blood stream will react in the same way and fizz out as little bubbles, which, if they get to your lungs, will cause you to die from an air embolism – the dreaded bends. But come up slowly, and you're grand – there's plenty to see on the way. Glorious arrangements of coral are everywhere and each piece is inhabited by shoals of the most fantastically coloured fish.

Back in the open water, a shoal of stripy barracuda fish goes past, followed by a turtle swimming most elegantly.

Just as the contents gauge reads empty and you are about to reach for the reserve valve, the surface is indicated by fronds of seaweed on the rocks. A quick clamber over the rocks, lugging the heavy bottle (still heavy although it is now empty), and you're back. The dive of a lifetime. 'Did you see this?' 'Did you see that?' we quiz each other. I don't mention the narcs or the funny-looking fish. We are all busy showing off how near we thought the hammerheads were to us. But later on that evening, looking through the fish book, trying to put names on the different brightly coloured fish that were darting through the coral, I was astounded to see a short thick green fish with a large bump on its head. Only occurs below forty metres, it said, and named it as a Napoleon wrasse (on account of its being so small and being full of its own importance, I suppose). 'Did you see this?' I casually asked the others. Would you believe it – everyone on that dive saw the Napoleon wrasse, and everyone thought they were hallucinating! Just as well the fish didn't hear the derogatory comments about its appearance or it might have acquired an inferiority complex.

That trip to dive in the Red Sea took place in 1979, when that part of Sinai was under the control of Israel after the Six Day War. We saw other parts of Israel too, besides the Red Sea coast. Much of that part of the world is in the Negev desert, where it hardly ever rains. But it had rained just before we arrived and there had been landslides. Deserts only come to life after rain and of course all the documentaries you see on television only show you the sudden flowering of the desert plants after the rain. We saw great sheets of yellow flowers, where dormant seeds had absorbed the rain and quickly germinated, grew, flowered and set seed again in a very short space of time. What the documentaries don't tell you is that hordes of flies appear after the rains too, and look for any food they can find to sustain themselves, while they mate and lay eggs that will survive in a dried-out state until the next rains. These flies are not particular about what they eat. They can visit the camp's makeshift toilet one minute and the lunch-time fish salad the next. One by one we succumbed: cramps, pains, the runs – just what you don't want on a diving holiday. Some of us were more resistant than others and got to go on most of the dives, but by the time we were scheduled to leave the Red Sea and go sightseeing, every one of us had had a dose or two. But we rallied. We were going to see and experience everything, and if we dived in the Red Sea, we were going to get into the Dead Sea as well.

The Dead Sea is one of the lowest points on earth, well below sea level, and the river Jordan runs into it. It doesn't overflow, however, because it is so hot that the rate of evaporation is very high. As much water evaporates every day as flows into the lake. But of course only pure water evaporates, and all the impurities are left behind. Whatever came in dissolved in the waters of the Jordan stays behind in the lake, and so the water becomes saltier and saltier. It is the saltiest sea in the world, and the water is very dense as well. You walk out into the lake, and by the time the water reaches your waist, it is able to support your weight. A few steps more and you are floating in a vertical position. You could lie back and read a paper, if you had a paper. Nothing can live in the water because it is so salty. Any living thing would shrivel up, as the liquid inside its body would try to achieve the same density as the water it was living in and so it would move out through its pores into the sea. Did we stay long enough there to shrivel up? Well, actually, no. We stayed in a very short period of time altogether. Very strong salty water is not the place to be after the affliction we had just suffered from, particularly considering that the toilet paper we had been using was more akin to sandpaper than double velvet. *Níl aon tóin tinn mar do thóin tinn féin,*[1] as they say. We spent a lot of time in the outdoor freshwater showers side by side – bending over to pick up the soap rather frequently.

---

1 The proverb is correctly *Nil aon tinteán mar do thinteán féin*, which means, 'There is no fireside like your own fireside' or 'Home, sweet home'. The version used here means 'There's no sore bottom like your own sore bottom.'

HUMMINGBIRDS: REAL AND PRETEND

HUMMINGBIRDS are extremely acrobatic flyers that only live in North and South America. They are beautiful, multicoloured birds and they feed on nectar. They can beat their wings up to eighty times a second and if this is filmed and the film subsequently slowed down, it can be seen that their wings move in a figure-of-eight fashion. The wings move so fast when they are flying that they produce a humming sound – like a fan. Hence their name: hummingbirds. This flamboyant, speedy way of moving their wings means that, uniquely among birds, they can fly backwards, or even, in their more flamboyant moments, upside down. They only eat nectar, which they extract from flowers with their long bills.

So imagine the scenario if you are a hummingbird. You are hungry and you want a meal. The only thing you can eat is nectar, which is meanly kept by the flowers deep down inside their petals. You are a bird, not an insect, so you cannot land on the flower to eat. So you have to hover in front of the open flower, beating your wings like the clappers, and insert your long bill right into the flower and drink the nectar from its depths. It's quite unsatisfactory, really. First of all, after all this manoeuvring to get exactly into the right position to drink, there is only a small amount of nectar to be had. Any hummingbird feeling even slightly peckish has to visit quite a few flowers to get a half-decent meal. And secondly, the blasted flowers keep the nectar hidden as far down as they possibly can, and quite often the hungry hummingbird gets its face all covered in dusty pollen, which the flowers always seem to have hanging inconveniently just at the entrance. It really covers a hummingbird's facial feathers. If only there was a way to get the nectar without all this dusty palaver!

Well, one hummingbird species, which thinks it's very smart, has recently discovered a way. The robber hummingbird which lives, among other places, in Costa Rica, has worked out that it can get at the nectar by going around the back of the flower. It flies to the bottom of the petals and pokes a hole with its beak directly through the petal bases into the nectar well. It can drink all the nectar directly through this back door, as it were, without getting its face and feathers all covered in that dusty pollen. This is such a superior thing to do that this hummingbird species gets all its nectar this way and in fact has concentrated all its efforts on one particular species of flower that is easily poked open through the petals at the back. Clever, or what?

Well, actually, it is not all that clever. Hummingbirds don't realise (and how could they, sure they can't read wonderful books that would tell them) that flowers reproduce by sending their pollen – their sperm, as it were – off to the female parts of other flowers via the hummingbirds' facial feathers. Hummingbirds are being used as go-betweens. As far as the flowers are concerned, they are paying for these sexual services by providing a meal – a practice not unknown to the human race. The pollen is taken to the next flower by the hummingbird in search of the next course in the meal, and is thrust on top of the ripe female part, as the hummingbird seeks the deeply hidden nectar. And so the flower is pollinated and can go on to produce seeds and, in the fullness of time, more flowers with more nectar for hummingbirds. But the smartypants hummingbird who has short-circuited the process is not so clever after all. The flower's bribe, the nectar, is being taken, but the price in pollen delivery is not being paid. Before long, these flowers will become extinct, as new seeds are not being made. And there will be no more wells of nectar for these hummingbirds to feed on, as hummingbirds are specific to a particular species of flower. Both are on the road to

extinction. Sometimes one can be too clever for one's own good.

Hummingbirds are fascinating birds. The smallest bird in the whole world is a particular species of hummingbird – the bee hummingbird – which is only two and a half inches long and weighs less than two grams, or one-sixteenth of an ounce. This is much smaller than our smallest bird, the goldcrest, which is a comparative monster, at three inches long and five grams in weight. In fact, the bee hummingbird is comparable with our large insects and has sometimes been confused with such by observers. Film-makers love hummingbirds because, as they hover in one place drinking nectar for a considerable period of time, relatively speaking, it is easy to focus on them and get wonderful pictures. As a result, they are among the film stars of the bird world and are very familiar to anyone who has ever spent any time at all looking at wildlife documentaries.

They are resident breeding species in North and South America, continents that are at least three thousand miles away from Europe. So why am I coming over all Discovery Channel describing them in loving detail if we are never going to have any of them in Ireland? Surely global warming is not advancing at such a rate that we can expect to be covered in tropical rainforest any time soon? Well, the truth is that listeners to the radio programme are reporting seeing hummingbirds in Ireland every summer. In fact, in 2003, a veritable deluge of them were seen in all parts of Ireland. How could they have got here? They are great show-offs when flying, but they haven't the stamina for the long haul. They could not fly three thousand miles across the ocean without refuelling regularly, and there are no nectar-filled flowers gracing the surfaces of the sea. The most they can manage is a five-hundred-mile hop across the Gulf of Mexico. Could it possibly be that our listeners are wrong? Are they hallucinating on their flower-filled patios on summer evenings? They definitely report hovering, backwards-flying nectar-drinkers approaching their nicotianas. And with the advent of these new camera mobile phones, they are taking their pictures and sending them in to us. What can they possibly be but humming-birds? What, indeed?

Well, they are actually moths – hummingbird hawk moths, so called because they look and behave like the real McCoys, the hummingbirds themselves. They are much smaller, of course, smaller even than the smallest hummingbird, at about one and a half inches, but that is not a problem when you have never actually seen a real hummingbird to compare it with. And they do fly backwards and forwards in front of flowers. Their long tongue is visible sticking into the flower, drinking nectar. And their wings beat so fast they make a humming noise. Their back wings are orange and their front wings brown, but all you can usually see is a brownish blur as they hover in front of the open flowers. Their bodies are quite thick and scaly, particularly at the back, where it looks superficially like feathers. But birds they are not, they are moths. It can be hard to convince the senders of the pictures that this is what they are, so sure are they that the camera never lies.

Hummingbird hawk moths are native to southern Europe, and they migrate northwards in summer – sort of a population expansion. Adults can arrive here in July in a good summer and, as they are day-flying moths, they can visit our garden flowers during sunshine, when we might well be out in the garden ourselves. They lay eggs on plants from the bedstraw family – flowers such as lady's bedstraw, or robin-run-the-hedge – which hatch into caterpillars, great green dramatic-looking things with pale blue lines along the sides and a yellow-tipped blue horn at the rear. These complete their life cycle here, so that there can be hummingbird hawk moths seen at Irish flowers right up to the end of September, or even later if the weather is glorious. They have no going-home mechanism; they came here on a one-way ticket. Further south in Europe, adults hibernate and survive the winter in this way, but here in Ireland, while hibernation is theoretically possible, it rarely happens.

So that's what our 'hummingbirds' are – moths. It is amazing that the same form and shape should evolve in two different continents in two completely separate forms of animal life, birds and moths, just to exploit a source of food. Both of them carry out pollination as an unwanted nixer, except of course for the robber hummingbird. There is no record yet of moths being able to turn into robbers and avoid the pollen.

TALKING WILD IN COSTA RICA

"WE'RE DOING A WORLD WILD SERIES" says Derek to me one day. 'Where would you like to make a forty-five-minute radio programme?'

Oh, the possibility of it all! Considering various scenarios kept me awake several nights. The Antarctic maybe, the Amazon basin, the Great Barrier Reef, among the head-hunters in Borneo, in Honolulu looking at volcanic activity and colonisation of recent islands... the mind boggled. It didn't boggle for too long, however. This was one of a radio series, not a big film documentary; there was a tiny budget – a shoestring – it had to be done in a week, or less, preferably; it had to be in English so that our listeners would understand it; it had to sound well, as there would be no visuals. And I was to make the programme contacts. So that put paid to Antarctica and Borneo and the Great Barrier Reef – even I couldn't speak underwater.

What would sound well on radio? Our dawn chorus programmes had been very well received. Where would the birds sing louder for longer? Where else but in America, where everything is bigger and better! Tropical rainforests have half of all the animal species on earth – there were bound to be a few that would sound good on the wireless. Tropical rainforest extends north into the continent of North America. We had a better chance of finding people speaking English there than in deepest Africa, or the Amazon basin. And when I remembered that a friend of a friend of mine was a zoologist in San José, the capital of Costa Rica, then the decision was easy. I would make my "world wild" debut among the rainforests of Central America, in Costa Rica to be precise.

Derek could only spare a few days towards the end of the week to make and record the actual programme itself. But it seemed to me an awful long way to go just for a few days, so by promising to pay for his flights and all his grub, I prevailed on my husband to accompany me there for an entire week. We landed in San José one dark night at the end of October, in the full knowledge, I must say, that it was the rainy season. However, it wasn't raining, nor was it the next morning, as we looked out over the city. It was like the nicest May morning you'd ever have in Ireland – sun shining, lovely blue sky with some white woolly clouds. There were big green mountains overlooking the city and the whole escapade looked full of promise. We had a driver and a van allocated to us for the week and, as Derek wasn't coming till Monday night, we had Saturday, Sunday and Monday to explore. We met Walter, our driver, at reception. The receptionist introduced us and said that Walter was at our disposal and was awaiting instructions. So we told her we wanted to visit the cloud forest in Monteverde. She told Walter, and off we went, bag and baggage.

Costa Rica is a country about the size of Ireland. It has the Atlantic on its east coast and the Pacific on the west. There is a great ridge of mountains like a backbone down the centre, which is part of the ridge that joins the Rockies to the Andes. The capital San José is – like Athlone – in the centre of the country. It lies about fifteen degrees north of the equator and the natural vegetation is forest. As the mountains rise, the temperature drops, so the type of forest depends on its position on the mountain. At the bottom are the hot, wet tropical forests and right at the top are the cloud forests of which Monteverde was one. There was a good road north for an hour or so, and then we came to the turn-off for Monteverde. The road deteriorated at once, and became a winding narrow track, which took several hours to negotiate and would not have accommodated anything bigger than our Hiace van. This is deliberate policy in Costa Rica, which depends a lot on eco-tourism and attracts rich tourists, mainly from North America. It is not in their interest to have large busloads of tourists swoop into their forest nature reserves, 'do' the place in a few hours and zoom off again. No value in that. You arrive half dead after your arduous journey, book into a nice chalet for two nights – dark six to six – and spend a whole day exploring the forest on foot and dining locally. A much more sustainable form of tourism than is seen in many another country. So we were there for two nights and, thanks to our early start with Walter, we had some daylight for our first exploration.

Well, was it crawling with wildlife? I'm sure it was, but how much did we see that first visit? The rainforest is dominated by broadleaved evergreen trees, so very little light penetrates to the forest floor. All the action takes place high up in the canopy, maybe fifty metres above our heads. We admired huge buttress roots, strangler fig trees that grew round ordinary, decent, unsuspecting trees and prevented them from expanding, lianas, epiphytes of all sorts, which are plants that grow way up on the branches of the main trees, bamboos, but few enough flowers. It was most amazing to stand there and see trees and ground shrubs and not to recognise a single one. I could see no species I knew until I rounded a corner and did a double-take. There, growing in a small light-filled spot, was a whole clump of busy Lizzies – the exact same plant that is so popular as a pot plant at home. This is where it lives in the wild – happy in cloud forest.

We heard lots of animal life, birds that sounded like a

squeaky door, and screeches from monkeys high overhead. The most exciting thing, I have to confess, was the hummingbird feeder back at the entrance building, where lots of very brightly coloured hummingbirds were drinking nectar out of specially designed bird feeders. We arranged a dawn guided walk and retired to our chalet greatly pleased with ourselves.

It was a different story at dawn the next day. The forest birds were in fine fettle, out exploring and looking for food as soon as it was light. They are mainly extremely brightly coloured birds, such as toucans, quetzals, ruddy pigeons, yellowish flycatchers, and they communicate by flashing their gaudy plumage at each other. It's a visual thing, so the sounds they make are secondary in the communication stakes. Such a disappointment! Such loud raucous calls! Nothing like the sweet melodious music of our woodlands at dawn in spring, when our mostly nondescript woodland birds communicate entirely by song. Nothing like the thrilling arias of our thrushes and blackbirds. Of course it was a great thrill to see the emerald-green plumage of the quetzal – a bird whose plumage was once so valued that it bedecked the garments of the emperor only – as it dined on wild avocados. We would get great sounds from the birds surely for the programme, but they would be bird racket rather than bird song. We went on our guided walk afterwards, and it was interesting to be on the receiving end of a tour for a change. And with expert eyes to notice and point out, we saw coati, white-faced monkeys, agouti, a coral snake – the dangerous one – and what seemed to be great big rat holes in the bank, but which turned out to be where the tarantula spiders live. And so it went for the day – every single thing was new. The butterflies were huge and dark violet in colour, with wings as big as our hands. Even the walk across to the chalet in the garden of the hotel was a field trip in itself.

Next day we were to go back to San José to meet Derek to make the programme. Walter took it into his head to show us the Pacific Ocean, so we detoured by Puntarenas on the west coast. Was there ever a town that could be described as the relics of auld dacency? Puntarenas had had its heyday, but it was now long past. It had been one of the elegant resorts visited by the cruise liners which sailed the Caribbean and came through the Panama canal just south of Costa Rica, but that was in the old days, and the cruise ships no longer come. It had the most splendid beach, with a whole line of magnificent buildings with balconies facing out to sea, but they were all faded, dilapidated, rusted. The ocean was great, though, my first time to see the Pacific. When we got back to the van, Walter, who seemed to consider this day as his treat, was waiting for us with our lunch at the ready. He had bought it from a roadside snack vendor and presented it to us with a flourish and an air of bestowing us with a great treat. It consisted of a banana leaf on which there was a mound of rice topped with tepid pork, then the pork crackling, then a salad of washed lettuce and tomato, topped with a dollop of mayonnaise. I thought weakly of all the advice we had been given about not eating from dodgy roadside stands, never eating tepid meat, particularly not pork, about avoiding washed salad and shunning mayonnaise-type dressings. I was only too acutely aware that even though I knew I was going to Costa Rica for ages, the exact dates were only settled at the last minute, and so there had been no time for any immunisations. I looked at Walter's beaming face and thought, 'What the hell!' and demolished the lot. It was tasty and I was hungry. In the van on the way back to San José, my husband, who had by now found Puntarenas in the guidebook, read aloud in sepulchral tones that Puntarenas was the only region in Costa Rica where cholera was still prevalent.

Halfway back, Walter's pager rang, and whatever message he got seemed to be important. But alas he had no English, and of course we had no Spanish. We stopped at a roadside café where the coffee was great. The girl serving the coffee which Walter had ordered came up and said 'Your friend says, your boss is not coming.' What? What friend, what boss? After much to-ing and fro-ing, it transpired that the pager had rung to say that Derek's plane had been held up by a hurricane in London and he would not be along till the next day. Well, at least we wouldn't be meeting him at the airport as unwitting carriers of cholera – we'd surely know by the next day what our fate was going to be.

You can't believe everything you read in the guidebooks.

Derek hopped off the plane all bright-eyed and bushy-tailed, half a day behind schedule and all set to reach the hot, wet tropical forest of La Selva before dark, so we firmly dismissed any thoughts of cholera and that was that. The hot rainforest was a completely different ecosystem from the cloud forest. Much hotter, much damper, full of flying insects which skidded off our insect-repelling cream as it slithered down our faces in the heat. We arranged to record the dawn sounds at five in the morning, the rain at midday and the night sounds after six. And that was how it was. The raucous birds duly performed as dawn broke and the moisture dripped off the trees. By nine o'clock the humidity was almost 100 per cent and we distracted ourselves looking at cacao trees with their long pods from which chocolate is made. Just before noon, there was an almighty howling from the trees above our heads – the howler monkeys who herald the rain. And then it rained – non-stop, in stair rods, for about three hours. The noise was incessant. And then it stopped and that was it. Except it wasn't. The water dripped continuously off the leaves for the rest of the day and you could nearly feel everything growing it was so hot and wet. Nothing is ever really dry there and clothes left hanging up for even a short length of time get covered in mould.

But we had a date with the darkness and, with Derek frantically trying to keep the recording gear dry and working, we sallied out when darkness fell. That is when the forests really came alive with sound. Such hot, wet forests are beloved of the amphibians, and there were frogs and toads everywhere. They were on the ground, up in the trees, along paths, behind stones, on leaves and all communicating with each other in one vast symphony of sound. Eric our guide could identify twelve different species calling at one time – poison arrow frogs, tree frogs, glass frogs, toads and salamanders. In all, forty species of amphibians occur here and none of them, it would seem, has taken a vow of silence. It was magnificent.

The Costa Rican government is now trying to replace the rainforest which had been cut down in a misguided effort to grow grass for beef, pineapples and now bananas, none of which has been a great commercial success in the protected, overpriced European markets. So they are turning the farmland back into rainforest in the hope that they will increase their tourist industry. This is not entirely a good news story, because where do the dispossessed farmers go and who compensates them for losing their land? We met some government officials, who assured us that all was well, and a dispossessed farmer who was still awaiting his compensation, which is to come, apparently, from the carbon taxes paid to Costa Rica by wealthy European and American countries for the use of their unneeded carbon allowance.

It's called Costa Rica – the rich coast – because when Christopher Columbus arrived, the inhabitants put on their best finery and went to welcome the visitor. And he, gazing upon their gold ornaments, thought, 'What a rich country

this must be!' and promptly slaughtered all the inhabitants. But there was no gold in Costa Rica; the people had earned their ornaments by trading with Guatemala. All the people there now are of Spanish origin; there are no native Costa Ricans left.

We left the following Saturday, coming home by Miami, where a British Airways hiccup forced us to stay overnight, and by Heathrow, where they were experiencing the worst rain and floods in decades. We saw more water flying in over Britain than we had seen in Costa Rica, where it rained every day for four hours.

DESIGNED TO KILL

NATURAL SELECTION for evolution is such a strong process that you would think that creatures have to be just right for the job or they would have long since gone to the wall. Any chink in the armour, any design fault, and there would have been a competitor waiting in the wings or indeed halfway to the spotlight to grab the opportunity and profit by the lapse. So if you look at bird design, say, you will see why the strong bills and talons of bird of prey have evolved and why they have such good binocular vision. If you are descending on a rabbit at great speed from the sky you want to be sure first of all that it is a rabbit and not a rock or an abandoned rubbish bag. Secondly, as you are only going to get one chance at it, you want to be sure that you can grab it in your outstretched talons and carry it off. Birds of prey that foul up don't get too many chances.

So, you might think that a bird that lives entirely on fish must be an excellent swimmer. But there are birds – birds that we know well in this country – that live entirely on fish and cannot swim at all. What could God have been thinking of when He designed them? Was it His little joke to make kingfishers fish-eaters and yet be unable to swim and live in the water?

The kingfisher must be one of the most recognised birds in this country. Often when I am introducing a lecture on wildlife – particularly when I feel that the audience fancies itself on its wildlife knowledge or feels that they know all this anyway – I will show them a selection of twenty common birds (of a possible total of over four hundred that have ever been recorded in this country), and there is often confusion between rooks and jackdaws and between starlings and blackbirds. Pied wagtails are often an unknown species (although there was great protest when the plane trees they roost in on O'Connell Street in Dublin's city centre were under threat). But the one bird that everyone without exception can recognise from the slide is the kingfisher. The turquoise feathers and the pointy bill are unmistakeable.

And yet, when questioned, many of the audience will never have seen a kingfisher in reality. But they are so, so photogenic that every year they grace some calendar or other and so impinge upon our consciousness. But did you realise that the reason why they are so photogenic is because they cannot swim? When the kingfisher feels peckish and would like a bit of dinner, what it has to do is perch on a viewing post that has a grandstand view of the river flowing below and wait for a manageable-sized fish to swim past. Then, when this happens, it dives into the water like an arrow, on to the unsuspecting fish, and grabs it in its beak. But of course it can't stay there in the water and eat its hard-won prize. It can't swim, and drowning is not part of the plan.

So it must immediately scramble back up to the surface of the water and fly back up to its watching perch to gobble its meal. And any half-alert photographer who has been hanging around the river bank has plenty of time to focus the camera on the perch and get a beautiful shot of the kingfisher with the water pearling off its feathers and the fish draped artistically in its bill. No wonder we can all recognise kingfishers!

But they are seen much more often in photos than in reality, because life is hard if you are a kingfisher in Ireland, where many of our rivers are arterially drained. Obviously, if you are going to catch your dinner by diving headlong into a river from a perch some distance above the water, it has to be a fairly deep river or you will brain yourself. Kingfishers are birds of mature rivers, not of fast-flowing, shallow mountain streams. And if having to catch fish without being able to swim wasn't bad enough, the design spec for where the nest is to be beggars belief – not in a tree, where you might reasonably expect it to be, or even on the bank of the river, hidden among vegetation like other water birds' nests. No, that would be much too easy. The kingfisher's nest is at the end of a tunnel excavated in the river bank and entered – wait for it – by diving under the water and coming up the tunnel, the end of which, you'll be glad to know, is above the water level. How do you excavate a tunnel of any sort without it collapsing in on top of you, never mind one in the bank of a flowing river? Miners use pit props and so too do the kingfishers, who make the best of their lot in life. The pit props in their case are the roots of the trees which grow on the banks of the river. The kingfisher tunnels alongside a large embedded root and this sustains the route to its nest.

So trees on river banks are vital to kingfishers. They must have a convenient branch overhanging the water on which they can perch to scan the water for passing dinners – bridge parapets are no good at all, much too frequented by *Homo sapiens* and his associated traffic – and they need convenient roots alongside which to excavate their tunnels. But trees along river banks are much less abundant since arterial drainage was invented.

On the face of it, arterial drainage is a great idea. In the natural state of affairs, the river flows through your holding and your fields on either side become flooded whenever the river floods and the water table rises. But now, suppose the river could be excavated and made deeper: the water table would then be lowered and your fields would not flood. In our early days of being members of the EEC (as it was called in those days), this was considered such a great idea that grants could be had to do this. And so enormous JCBs were brought alongside the rivers and the beds scooped out and dumped in heaps on the river banks. To get access along the river, any trees in the way had to be removed. Of course this wasn't great news for the fish who used the gravels in the river beds for spawning, as this was all upset, but the rivers did recover after five years and fish came down again from areas higher up, which hadn't been drained, or else the rivers were restocked by anglers. But the poor kingfishers! They could hardly get leave of absence for five years while their devastated river bank recovered somewhat. They could hardly go to Tenerife on their holidays or start eating something else and making nests on top of the spoil heaps – and so their numbers crashed. The fields grew crops and supported cattle and enlarged the butter and grain mountains in Europe (remember those?) and our poor kingfishers paid the price.

If ever we need a quality mark for the river, a gold star as it were, it should definitely be the kingfisher. Not only will there be fish in the river if we see kingfishers, but the banks will be in good nick, there will be trees along the bank, there will be nice, undisturbed stretches and pollution will be minimal.

The kingfisher is not the only fish-eating bird that cannot swim. The heron comes into this category too. At least the heron has long legs and can wade about in the shallows, hoping to encounter a fish. And it isn't confined to fish.

Herons are partial to frogs and, I'm sorry to say, the eggs and nestlings of other water birds, if they can nab them while unprotected. But fish forms a main part of the heron's diet and really this bird is the living example of the truth of the expression 'Everything comes to him who waits'. The patient heron standing motionless in the shallows of a river or at the edge of a lake, its long grey neck and body often merging with the vegetation near by, is a familiar sight.

A measure of our familiarity with it is the number of names by which it is known in Irish – *corr éisc, corr ghlass, corr mhóna, corr riasc* as well as pet names like *Máire Fhada* and *Síle na bPortach*. Indeed, it is often called the crane, and in Irish the names given above refer also to the crane. Up to the 1600s, cranes were plentiful in Ireland as well as herons. They were much taller than herons, but they also frequented marshy places, particularly the raised midland bogs. They became extinct here in the seventeenth century, but the name in both Irish and English is often still applied to the heron.

The heron is actually quite well designed for catching fish, if you allow for the fact that it cannot swim. It stands patiently for hours in the water, hoping a fish will swim over its feet. The poor deluded fish swimming along thinks that it is a nice shady tree and swims right in under the shade. Quick as a flash, the rapier-like beak goes in, but in fact the heron does not impale the unfortunate fish on the end of its sharp bill. How would it get it off again, considering it has no hands? No, the heron has to wait all day pretending to be a tree in the hope of luring a fish and then when one comes, it has to catch it in an instant and swallow it head first. If it swallows it tail first the scales will be rubbed the wrong way and the heron will choke. It surely has to know whether the fish is coming or going.

The heron flies home in the evening with ponderous wing flaps and its long legs sticking out behind it in a most recognisable fashion. Amazingly for such a big bird, it nests in colonies – called heronries – at the tops of tall trees, and it has the ugliest chicks imaginable. Only their mother could love them. And did you know that herons can tell the time? But they can't read. At least this is the case for the herons in the Phoenix Park in Dublin. Some of them have copped that it is much easier to cadge a meal by hanging around the sea lion and the penguin enclosure in Dublin Zoo than by standing in the Liffey all day at Islandbridge. So come five to three in the afternoon, they begin to gather in the trees around this part of the zoo to apply for fishy handouts. And the keepers there are kind to them and fling the odd mackerel in their direction, as they dispense the food to the sea lions and penguins. But occasionally, feeding will not, after all, take place at three o'clock, and there will be a notice up to this effect, so that the public needn't wait in vain for the feeding spectacle. But the poor herons assemble anyway and look forlornly down over the area, unaware of – or perhaps unable to read – the notice. I wonder how long they wait. Is their patience as elastic in the trees over the sea-lion lake as it is in the river shallows?

It is certainly more elastic than mine, as I never waited long enough to see them depart all disappointed.

Our listeners don't always love herons, however, particularly if they have just cleared their garden pond of goldfish. Brightly coloured foreign fish in a shiny pond in a built-up area must be really easily seen by the sharp-eyed aerial heron. All it has to do is land in the garden, walk a few steps around the pond and pick out the brightly coloured prey and swallow them (head first of course). You can't really expect them not to. But our listeners want their foreign exotic fish and are not impressed with the close-up views of a wild Irish heron landing in their back garden just beyond the kitchen window and providing excellent birdwatching material. How can we deter them? they plead in unison. There is a theory that you could place a strand of fishing line around the pond at a height of, say, a foot above the ground, and the heron would not see this and would walk into it and be scared off. But certain herons specialising in garden-pond raiding seem to be able to step elegantly over the strand of fishing line and hit the jackpot. Maybe you'd need two or three parallel strands, but then you'd probably fall over them yourself when you dashed out at the start of a shower of rain to bring in the clothes and kill the goldfish anyway by landing on top of them.

Another fish-eating bird that cannot swim is the osprey. Now, if you want a bit of drama, the osprey is your man. This is a bird of prey, known also as a fish hawk, although it cannot swim a stroke itself. It flies over a lake or estuary, and when it spots the fish swimming in the water, down it plummets and grabs the fish in its talons and flies off with it.

Ospreys are migratory birds, which spend their winters in west Africa. Some of them at least used to spend their summers with us. There are some who say that the drawing of an eagle in the ninth-century Book of Armagh looks more like an osprey than an eagle. However, there is archaeological evidence as well, so we really don't have to depend on the birdwatching skills of a ninth-century monk to know that we once had them in residence. But not now: gamekeepers in the mid-eighteenth century saw off the last of them, blaming them for their diminishing supplies of fish.

Ospreys are resident in Scotland, the species having become re-established there in 1954, and they live in Scandinavia too. They breed there every summer and fly to and from Africa in spring and autumn. Sometimes their aviation route takes them over Ireland, so it is not beyond the bounds of reason that they are sometimes seen here. In fact, they can hunt and feed here if they feel hunger pangs *en route*. But if you didn't know that, if you had never heard of a bird of prey which caught fish with its feet, what would you make of the story, which made the Mayo newspapers, of a four-pound salmon that crashed through the roof of a house, breaking the roof tiles and shattering itself into smithereens? The newsroom in RTÉ were amazed and rang me to see if I could offer them and the listeners an explanation at one-thirty in the afternoon. No better woman! They were able to confirm that there had been no aircraft in the area at the time, so it wasn't a helicopter pilot's lunch. When I suggested that it might be an osprey, as it was the migrating time of year, and a four-pound salmon might have been just a tad too heavy to keep aloft for long, they were plainly astonished.

'Could it not have been dropped by a seagull?' they asked.

'How could a seagull with webbed feet carry a salmon?' says I.

'Perhaps in its bill,' they falteringly suggested, 'though, perhaps not...' they trailed off.

'No,' I pontificated, 'it was definitely an osprey.'

Although in fact, nobody had seen such a bird or indeed anything dropping a fish on the roof. You would think, if you heard an almighty crash on your roof, you'd rush out and look up to see what caused it. And further disappointment – the salmon was so shattered it couldn't even be eaten. Its size was determined purely by the remains of its head.

Derek Mooney told me later that he had been told it was common practice for aeroplane pilots to hurl salmon out of aeroplane windows as a joke. Out of sealed and pressurised plane cabins? Come on, Derek, whose leg is being pulled?

BEAUTIFUL WATER POLICE

THE FIRST TIME I ever spoke about wildlife on radio was in the 1970s to the late John Skehan, he of the wonderful voice. I had been invited on to say what was happening in the world of wildlife at that time of year and I happened to mention dragonflies. What were they and why should anyone be interested in them? John wanted to know. I was working in An Foras Forbartha in the Biological Records Centre at the time, and, while I had some class of information from the public on mammals and butterflies, I had none at all on dragonflies. I felt this was an opportunity to encourage people to observe and record them and send me in records. Foolish me! How would the public know one from another – or that they were even dragonflies in the first place? John, not unreasonably, asked me. Why were they important anyway?

And indeed almost thirty years later, the same questions might still be asked. My postbag often brings questions about and indeed photographs of the large dragonflies, with the inevitable question, 'What are these and what good are they?'. Well, they are indicator species, no less, to give them the full benefit of modern jargon. In other words, they are extremely fussy creatures that will only live in the cleanest water bodies. Their young and teenage stages – the nymphs – last for several years and then they crown a reticent life with a flamboyant and exuberant adult flying stage. Anyone with an iota of observational skills, if they are near fresh water at all, cannot fail to notice dragonflies in flight. We have at least twenty-four species in Ireland and they fly, one or other species of them, all summer long. The earliest of them is on the wing by May, and you may still observe flying dragonflies at the end of September.

Unlike butterflies, dragonflies are carnivores and all stages of them, young and adult, will dine on their less fortunate fellow-creatures. Butterflies are herbivorous, as we know to our cost when we gaze ruefully at the remains of our prized nasturtiums, but they only drink as adults – no eating. Dragonflies, on the other hand, dine on underwater creatures during the two years or so they live down there. Then, when they become adults and get wings, they fly around catching and eating aerial prey very efficiently.

I wonder does it taste very different and how do the dragonflies know that this is what they must eat from now on? Nobody teaches them anything – it is all hard-wired in, they know all this by instinct. (We, on the other hand, know very little from instinct and have to be taught almost everything. Either we learn vast amounts or we are slow learners, but it takes us at least fourteen years to get a working knowledge of life – and that's only an average figure.)

Dragonflies are part of the water police that monitor conditions in our lakes and rivers. A rummage through stones in a fast-flowing stream will reveal the nymphs clinging to the undersides. They are dull, greyish creatures, only noticeable because they move. They have six legs, three tails and two antennae. They lie there on the rock, grey and colourless, giving no indication of the glorious, exciting creatures they will metamorphose into during the second spring of their lives. They look innocuous enough from above – two large eyes and, in the case of the smaller, damselfly species, three tails, which are actually their gills, through which they extract the oxygen from the water. But if you look at the head from underneath, you may see that they have the most ferocious and efficient mouth. Their lower lip is like no ordinary lip you have ever seen – it is modified into an enormous, hinged food-catching apparatus. Just imagine a very long lower lip with two claws, called palps, at the outside end of it. It is folded in two and kept neatly under the dragonfly's head, where it acts as a mask concealing its face, all but its eyes. It walks around smartly on the bed of the river, hiding its real intentions behind this false face, looking for food. It spies a little worm some distance away. It flips out its lower lip, straightening the hinge to make it twice as long, and grabs the hapless worm in the claws strategically positioned at the end of its lip. Yum.

It grows big and strong quite quickly, and soon is too big for its skin. It can only grow by bursting its coat or moulting, and there are usually between ten and fifteen moults in the nymph's life. Sort of like birthdays, I suppose, each one marking a stage of growth. If there is lots of food available, they grow very fast and the interval between moults is short enough. In poor, cold waters it can take up to five years for a dragonfly to complete all the moultings. Surely a case, if there was ever one, where stuffing yourself at every opportunity can shorten your life.

At each moulting the creature becomes bigger, its eyes get larger in proportion, and wings begin to develop underneath the wing cases high up on its back. Eventually the nymph knows that this impending moult it feels coming on is the big one (they must feel something special, because they've hardly counted all the other ones), and they leave the water and climb up on the vegetation above.

This last moult changes them completely from a wingless, nondescript, underwater nymph to a glorious brightly coloured flying creature. It happens at dawn some bright summer's morning and the whole thing only takes a few hours at the most – unlike the butterfly, who can spend months in a cocoon changing from caterpillar to adult. Once the dragonfly is on the vegetation, it has a short rest, no doubt to recover after such unusual exertion. It then splits the skin at the back of its head and removes its head and upper body from it – rather like removing a balaclava by tearing it up the back. More rest, then, before the final, Trojan effort, which is splitting the rest of the skin covering the abdomen and pulling that out (think of getting out of your sleeping bag sideways). Adult dragonflies are much bigger than nymphs and have wings, so inflation has to be the next step. The dragonfly expands by pumping blood around its body and out along the veins of its wings. If you happen to see such an emerging dragonfly early one morning as you stroll by the lakeside, it is nothing short of magical to see how this thing expands to a full-sized dragonfly. It holds out its expanding and hardening wings until they dry off and with one mighty bound, it then flies off to explore the world. It takes a few days for the colour to develop but when it does, these are among the most brightly coloured of all our flying insects. Their eyes can be bright blue or emerald green or blood red, and they bulge out enormously on either side of the head. Each eye is as big as the head itself and is exceedingly efficient at spotting movement of any sort. It is very hard to catch adult dragonflies – they say black nets are better than white nets, but luck and speed are better still.

Their bodies develop the most beautiful colours – the

males in particular, wouldn't you know. Even the very words used to describe them by normally sober scientists not given to flights of fancy are compelling – azure, Prussian blue, crimson, bronze, amber, emerald green, apple green, metallic green, saffron, ash grey. They fly about so very obviously in their gleaming colours and yet they are prey to very few predators. Their supremely efficient eyes detect any untoward movement in their direction and with four independently moving wings they are the fliers *par excellence*, being able to wheel and turn and dart to avoid capture. This dexterity also makes them extremely deadly predators. They are still carnivores, still starving, needing lots of energy for this continuous fast flight, and so they hawk up and down over rivers and waterways in hot pursuit of midges, mosquitoes and flies of all sort. Once they get within striking distance, they zoom up all their legs together, forming a basket in which they catch the prey. They can then eat it leisurely, with their toothed jaws. (The toothed lip seems to be a feature only of the nymphal stage, which is just as well, really, since the main aim in life of adult dragonflies is to find a mate and settle down in life, and really could you have a meaningful relationship with a partner with a protruding toothed lower lip?)

Flying up and down the river ostensibly looking for food allows the males to show off their sartorial beauty and their boy-racer flying skills, and it is not long before they are selected by a discriminating female as the love of their lives. Of course the male was expecting to be chosen and he has prepared himself very carefully for this moment. Insects in general have their reproductive structures at the tips of their abdomens and mate by pressing these tips together, as even a cursory glance at mating butterflies will illustrate. But nothing so mundane for our dragonflies. Uniquely among insects, the male dragonfly has reproductive organs on the second and third segments of its abdomen *as well as* the regular one on segment nine down at the end of the body. So, in the equivalent, I suppose, of tanking up with a few pints before going out on the pull, he transfers sperm from the opening at segment nine back up to segments two and three. He flexes the muscles in his claspers at the very end of his body – they are going to get great use and he must be sure they're up to the job – and off he goes. The first female that lovingly approaches, he grasps her firmly with his claspers by the back of the neck and they fly along in this firm embrace. The female has to curve her body right under his until her reproductive parts, which are in the right place at the end of her body, touch his segments two and three and pick up the sperm so thoughtfully deposited there by himself, who had all this planned. No spur of the moment falling in love here. But that is not the end of it. The sperm makes its way into her body and immediately fertilises the eggs she has ready there. She soon feels the urge to lay these eggs and no better man to help than himself, who still has his claspers firmly around her neck. Off they fly together, still in tandem, until they reach a likely-looking spot. They can see the suitable vegetation under the surface of the water below. And down they go. He flies right down and immerses her in the water just at the exact spot beside the plant. She quickly cuts a slit in the plant and inserts an egg while no doubt he whistles nonchalantly and looks at his watch. But soon he gets the nod, he hauls her up and flies off again to another likely plant. There he dunks her in again and waits while she does the business. Imagine the bonds of trust there must be between the pair: she has to be sure that he will actually pull her up when the job is done and not leave her below to drown, and he has to be sure that she will actually lay the eggs he has contributed his sperm to and not fake it. A whole pleasant afternoon is spent in this occupation – dragonflies can be seen flying in tandem for up to five hours in suitable habitats.

The eggs duly hatch out under the water and the nymphs climb down the plant into the depths to live chasing smaller creatures. They face a lifetime of fifteen moults before in their turn ascending to the upper world of flight and sunshine and colour. Meanwhile, the amorous parents have another two or three weeks of glorious life, maybe longer in exceptional summers. Since we have at least twenty-four species, there are always some on the wing on any good summer's day in suitable habitat.

So I gave John Skehan a glowing account of the riveting behaviour of dragonflies. And was I inundated with records? Well, no, actually – perhaps observers were so taken with the wonders they were looking at that they forgot to make records. However, there was a source – a wonderful source – of records, which had just come to my attention. Cynthia Longfield of Castlemary in Cloyne in County Cork had been in communication with the Centre and had offered to make her records available. In those days (the 1970s), I had no idea who Cynthia Longfield was. She sounded old on the phone (in the event she was eighty) and she wanted to give Irish dragonfly records to the Biological Records Centre – that's all I knew. Would I come down to Cork to make arrangements for this? Amazingly, I got official permission to go – expenses, mileage, the lot – and off I went, with an appointment to meet Miss Longfield at three o'clock in the afternoon. She lived in Park House in Cloyne and I didn't have to ask for directions. It was the big house in the area, although apparently a smaller house than the original Castle Mary, which was burned down in the 1920s during the War of Independence. I was ushered in by Cynthia's assistant, nearly as venerable as Cynthia herself, and asked if I would take tea. Cynthia received me in her drawing room, a woman of presence and vigour, with a commanding voice in the tones of the gentry. I was served afternoon tea – I still remember the green china – and Cynthia immediately began to discuss dragonflies. Well, *discuss* is hardly the word, as I had nothing of moment to say to this redoubtable woman, who had spent her life working on dragonflies, who had discovered quite a few new to science and who even had one species called after her. 'It is all to do with penis size and shape you know,' she declared firmly, when I made some inane remark about how would you tell a new species from one that might be similar. I withdrew to more familiar territory – to me anyway. How would we get all the records up to Dublin? They were interspersed throughout all her notes and papers, she said; she would have to go through them all and extract them. Writing was not easy for her now, with arthritis. There must be some modern way.

Well, there was. Dictaphones. I looked at her doubtfully and wondered would she be able to load the little tapes, press the right buttons, record her material so that it could be typed out later, keep track of what she had recorded, and post them all up to Dublin. Oh, the impertinence of callow youth! There was I thinking these thoughts of a woman who (I subsequently found out) had crossed Africa on her own – a woman traveller in 1934 – from Mombasa to Nairobi, to Uganda, to the source of the Nile, to the Belgian Congo, to Lake Tanganyika, through northern and southern Rhodesia to Cape Town five months later. She had visited South America, where, as well as collecting, she nonchalantly informed the Bolivians that the Paraguayan army was on the way to invade. She had crossed the Rockies on horseback. She had collected in south east Asia. She'd sailed to the Galapagos. Uncharacteristically – and fortunately – for me, I didn't embark upon a whole explaining process about how to work the machine, but left it there with the tiny tapes and hoped for the best. And every week the tapes arrived in Dublin with Cynthia's voice loud and clear on each one, wonderfully enunciating the records, spelling out the species' Latin names and giving precise locations of where they were recorded. Each one took up where the other left off, and, over the weeks, I was able to have the records typed up and to make the maps. She proofread every one and checked over each map. Of the records in that first atlas produced in 1978 – *Provisional Atlas of Dragonflies in Ireland* – over 80 per cent were hers. She continued working and became the first fellow of the British Dragonfly Society in 1983. But I never met her again and it was to be 1991 before I fully realised the impact she had made on the scientific world, when I read her obituary following her death at the age of ninety-five.

CHAPTER NINE

SLITHERY THINGS IN THE RIVERS

WHEN ST PATRICK banished the snakes from Ireland, his brief must have extended only over the land, because there are certainly long, narrow, sinuous creatures in our rivers, lakes and indeed sometimes in our holy wells. Chief among these are eels, which are extremely common creatures. Did you know that eels are catadromous, which is the direct opposite of anadromous, which is what salmon are? In case these words don't come tripping naturally off the tongue, what it means in simple English is that salmon are born, and eventually themselves breed, in fresh water, but do all their feeding and growing in the salty sea, whereas eels feed and grow fat here in our freshwater systems, but breed and are born in faraway salty seas.

Eels first become apparent as elvers, tiny worm-like creatures two or three inches long, that appear in our rivers in spring. They arrive in from the sea and, in the main, swim up the rivers. But if the going gets tough, they are not averse to ceasing to swim, and getting out and walking, or at least slithering, across the wet grass to an adjoining pond, or indeed holy well, where they sometimes appear after a particularly wet night. They can be eaten at this stage: collected in buckets, washed in salty water, fried in bacon fat and eaten as they are, heads, guts, skins and all, just as deep-fried whitebait is eaten. In fact, around the Severn River in England, where eels are particularly abundant, they have elver-eating competitions – who can eat the most in the shortest time? (Apparently the record stands at a pound in a minute.)

They come out at night to feed on whatever insect larvae they can find, and spend the summer days lying motionless in the water, apparently sunbathing, no less. They spend long summers in our rivers and lakes, feeding and growing big. They soon change from the tiny glass elvers they arrived as, to yellow eels which are not so good to eat. They take years and years to grow up. Given that they are three years old when they arrive, they will spend at least another nine years, if they are male, or twelve, if they are female, before they reach puberty. They hibernate each winter in the mud in the bed of the rivers and emerge again each

April to continue the growing process. As they approach maturity, a great change comes over them. They become fatter, their eyes grow bigger and their skin changes colour from yellow to a purplish black. They are now known as silver eels and they are remarkably good to eat at this stage, if you like their rich, rather oily flesh. They are particularly good smoked, however – meaty and crisp – with the added advantage that you don't have to kill them yourself, you can buy them ready prepared if you want them like this. They are not sold fresh in any fish shop I know – Irish people are not particularly partial to them in the southern part of the island, although there is a great eel fishery in Toomebridge, where the Bann River leaves Lough Neagh. There are eel traps on rivers down here too, but the eels caught are all for export, to Holland and Denmark, where they are greatly prized. In Zeeland in the Netherlands they even make a special bread roll with an eel curled up inside. If you want an eel here, you can go to where there is an eel trap and ask for one. But you'll get it alive and killing it and preparing it for cooking is not for the faint-hearted. You can try chopping off its head with a cleaver and then cutting its body into lengths. But the bits all move by themselves in a disconcerting manner in the frying pan for a while afterwards and you still have to deal with the skin. The skin of an eel is so tough it was once used to hold the two sides of a threshing flail together, so you should really try to get rid of it before cooking. The classic way to deal with a live eel to prepare it for cooking is as follows. (Are you paying attention? You never know when you may be called upon to carry out this operation.) You kill it by inserting a skewer through the back of its head and then you hang up the dead eel on a strong hook for the skinning operation. With a Stanley knife and a brand new blade you cut a circular cut all around, just below the head. Put back the (washed) Stanley knife in the toolbox and take out the pliers. Pull the skin down, away from the cut, with the pliers, until you have it loosened all the way round. Then sprinkle the loosened skin with salt to get a grip and pull it down, as if you were removing the tight football socks from your small son's legs and feet. It will come off reluctantly and with great difficulty. You may need another lash at it with the pliers so don't put them back until you've got it all off. Then – if you don't need it to repair your threshing flail – you can discard the skin along with the head and whatever entrails you can find. You can then cook it in the French style (in a red wine sauce as a *matelote*), in the Dutch style (with apples), in the German style (as Hamburg eel soup), in the Belgian style (with sorrel and spinach), grill it like the Italians do, have it with spuds and white sauce like the Danes, in an eel pie as the English fancy it when they are not making jellied eels, but try as you will, you will not find any traditional recipes for eel in this part of Ireland. There is an Irish name for it – *eascú*, the hound of the waterfall – but it was considered fare only for the cat, as it was thought to be a dirty fish that fed on offal. Along the shores of Lough Neagh, the fishermen would eat what they could not sell and would always parboil the eel pieces first to get rid of the oil before frying them. Nowadays the fishing rights have passed from individuals and the eels are exported. However, do try smoked eel if you can get your hands on it. It is a revelation.

Anyway, the fat silver eels are on the way out. Having eaten and grown fat in our fresh waters for years and years, they are now overcome with an urge to swim downriver towards the sea. They enter the salt water and they never feed again. The fat they have put on is their fuel for their journey all the way across the Atlantic to the Sargasso Sea in the Gulf of Mexico. And it is there, among the seaweeds, that they mate and die. It must be, because that is where the baby elvers come from, although the adult eels have never been actually recorded breeding there. A Danish biologist, Johannes Schmidt, first found the tiniest eel larvae there as recently as 1922. Before that it was thought that they came from dew drops! Presumably this journey to and from the breeding grounds is very ancient and must date from the time when America and Europe were very close to each other. They separated by continental drift and as the distance between them grew further and further, so it took the baby eels longer to reach European fresh water. Some of them go north to America and only take a year to get there. But they don't choose where to go. It depends on what ocean current they get caught in where they will end up.

We have a second snake-like creature in our river – the

lamprey. Richard Collins, my colleague on the radio programme, hails from Limerick, and he speaks of the fearsome reputation the lamprey had when he was growing up. It was reputed to be of considerable length, to live by sucking blood, particularly that extracted from the legs of tasty young lads swimming in the Shannon. If one got stuck to your leg or thigh it would lock its teeth on to the skin and start sucking blood. Only fire would dislodge the monster, a lighted match applied to its belly. While this did not happen to Richard, or indeed anyone of his acquaintance, it certainly livened up a swim in the river, where every brush against a submerged weed could be a possible lamprey approach.

Should I enhance a good story with the facts? No better woman! After all, we had the sea to swim in, in Clogherhead when I was young, and my childhood was never troubled by lamprey nightmares. They are the most primitive group of vertebrates – animals with backbones – and they have been around for hundreds of millions of years. There are indeed several species to be encountered in our rivers by unwary swimmers. The biggest one is the sea lamprey, which has a life cycle like the salmon. It is born in fresh water, goes to sea to get big and fat, and then returns to the rivers from the sea to spawn and die. These can be quite substantial creatures and can grow up to three feet in length. And they *are* vampires: they are parasitic fish and live by fastening themselves on to other fish in the sea and sucking their blood. They have evolved in shape just to be able to this. They have only a backbone, no other bones, and their head is entirely a mouth. They attach themselves to the selected fish by their large suctional mouth and then stick their circular teeth into the poor creature's flesh. They then rasp and suck away, drinking the fish's blood for its meal. They do drop off eventually, but the victim is never the same afterwards and doesn't thrive; smaller victims die from the attack.

When they have reached maturity in the sea, lampreys come in to breed in fresh water. They congregate in estuaries before heading upriver to spawn, and it is here that they can be caught by fishermen. This only happens in those countries where they feature on the menu – not in Ireland, of course, needless to remark. But in Portugal they are caught at the mouth of the Minho river, and of course the French eat them too (what do the French not eat?). They are caught around Bordeaux and made into a *conserve de lamproie à la bordelaise*. No doubt there is a special claret to go with it. They smoke and eat it in Finland too.

Those that escape the nets of the gourmet fishermen come into the rivers to breed and then die having done so. The resultant larvae feed on detritus and small organisms here for a while, before metamorphosing and heading off to sea to feast on cod, salmon and anything else they can lay their jaws on. So, no dangers to the thighs of young river swimmers from the sea lamprey – it only feeds at sea.

The next species of lamprey is the river lamprey. This is a different species, much smaller than the sea lamprey, and it spends most of its life in rivers. However, it does venture to sea just for one year during its life cycle. It then returns to our rivers and continues to live and feed here until spawning time comes. It attaches itself to trout in our waters and does its horrible sucking thing to them. Its jaws are not actually strong enough to penetrate human skin, but I suppose if you caught a trout with one of these stuck to it, you might be inclined to think that it could. When it is not feeding, it attaches itself to a stone at the bottom by the sucker – sort of parks itself – to prevent itself from being washed downstream. In fact, there is a curious tale of fishermen exploiting this very behaviour to catch them. They insert nets on long poles carefully under the stones and scoop them up with the lamprey still attached to the stone by its mouth.

They were partial to the lampreys in Britain as well as to eels. The Severn used to be famous for lampreys and the city of Gloucester on the banks of the river was famed for its lamprey cuisine. The good burghers of Gloucester used to keep well in with the monarchy by presenting the sovereign with a *lamprey pye* on special occasions. In 1977 the tradition was revived for the Queen's silver jubilee. Twelve lampreys were used in the pie, which weighed twelve pounds upon completion and was a foot in diameter and six inches deep. It was duly dispatched to London by mayoral car upon a 'handsome wooden plinth' that had been made specially. Of course the event was covered by the media who got to eat 'ones that were made earlier' in

Gloucester and, sceptical though they were, they all 'declared it to be delicious'. There is no record, good, bad or indifferent, of what Her Majesty's reaction was, but I didn't hear that she got one for her golden jubilee.

The third type of lamprey encountered in our rivers is the smallest one – the brook lamprey. It is the same design as the others, all mouth and sucker when it is fully developed as an adult, but this one only uses its sucker to move stones around to make a nest when it is spawning. It doesn't feed at all as an adult, just looks out for a mate, sorts the nesting site, spawns and dies soon after. The larvae hatch out and look more like earthworms than fish. They live for four years in the mud, feeding quite respectably on dead plant material, and then develop into non-dining adults. These never go to sea, but spend all their lives in rivers and scarcely deserve the fearsome reputation their bigger cousins more deservedly have – at least if you are a fish.

There is another interesting creature that lives in our freshwater habitats and occasionally we get queries from listeners about them. They report that they have found prawn-like creatures in their river or lake and wonder how this can be, so far from the sea. These shellfish are not prawns at all, of course, but a lookalike that lives in fresh water – the crayfish. Ireland, believe it or not, is a stronghold for these animals, because much of our freshwater habitat is remarkably clean. Although they are edible and indeed very nice to eat, there was never any history of eating crayfish here. They were never caught commercially and hardly anyone caught them for themselves. They are one of the very few invertebrate species that are now protected under recent environmental legislation. They are protected under The Wildlife Act, in its latest amendment, and fourteen named sites where they occur – nine lake complexes and five stretches of river – were declared to be Special Areas of Conservation (SACs) under the Habitats' Directive.

They live in lime-rich waters where the pH is high and where there is plenty of cover for them in the form of stones and underwater vegetation. They look like a Dublin Bay prawn. They have a strong meaty tail, which they flex in order to move and two quite massive claws, which they use to defend themselves and grab their prey. They can live for up to fifteen years, getting bigger and bigger each year, and can reach up to four inches in length. They reach maturity when they are about three, and mate every year after that. Mating is a weird and wonderful process when looked at from a human perspective. The males fight among each other over the females, and the strongest gets to choose the lady. He picks someone his own size or smaller, never bigger. After a certain amount of wrestling, he deposits a sperm package on her abdomen and retires, job done now till next year. She has to go around with this thing stuck to her until, some days later, she finally produces a substance that will dissolve the package. She then lays her eggs, which are fertilised by the sperm now released from the package. But that is not the end of that. No, horrors! The fertilised eggs now become attached to her swimming legs and she is stuck with carrying them around. She has to hide away until they hatch, *eight* months later, in June, and she hardly feels like eating at all during this time. Talk about morning sickness! Eventually they do hatch and drop off and, with her appetite miraculously restored, she goes on a feeding binge. The babies, so carefully minded as eggs, are now left to take their chances and they grow fast, moulting their hard shell as they grow – maybe up to twenty times in their first year. No one wants to chew a hard crayfish, but they are fair game when they are in a moult, and lots of things have a go at them – fish, other invertebrates and – shock! horror! – even other crayfish.

They used to be very common all over Europe. All the rivers and lakes had them, and need I say they featured strongly in the culinary repertoires of France, where they are called *écrevisses*, and in English cookery, where recipes are preceded with instructions on how to catch them. Apparently you use a freshly butchered sheep's head as bait. You leave this in the water overnight and when you haul the grisly object out next day, the scavenging crayfish have crawled right into the skull and can easily be retrieved to go into your crayfish soup, for which you will apparently need two hundred. But the best recipe which includes crayfish is the original one for chicken Marengo. Napoleon was just after winning the battle of Marengo in 1800 in the southern part of Piedmont in Italy. He was starving, as you would be, so he ordered his chef to cook a sumptuous

repast. The chef, needless to remark, hadn't been able to spend the day over a hot stove – in fact, he had nothing to cook at all. He went out to see what he could scrounge in the locality. He managed to acquire a chicken, some garlic, wild mushrooms and some crayfish in the local stream (a resourceful sort of chef, you might think) and Napoleon was always good for a bottle of wine, so the dish chicken Marengo was allegedly created. There is a recipe listing all these ingredients dating from 1773, and the Parisian restaurant *Trois Frères Provençaux* claims that it invented the dish for the benefit of Napoleon's generals upon their victorious return from battle. Maybe if we won more battles and were used to being victors there would be such dishes as Clontarf delicacy, Castlebar mouthful, Benburb stew or Athlone pie.

HOW TO BOIL AN EGG IN A SOCK

ONE OF THE PERKS of doing a wildlife radio show is that occasionally, very occasionally, one gets to leave these shores and go and see wildlife in other climes. Over the ten-year period that *Mooney Goes Wild* has been on the air, I got to go in an aeroplane four times in a work capacity. The first time was in 2000, when we spent an October week in Costa Rica. In 2002, we went to visit wetlands in Wales and in December 2003 we went to the Natural History Museum in London. In February 2004, Iceland was duly visited. All of these trips were memorable in their ways, but Iceland was something else.

This island, about halfway across the Atlantic, is a little

bit bigger than Ireland and lies just south of the Arctic Circle. What would it be like in February? Would it be absolutely freezing, so that we'd have to dress like Shackleton? The newspapers were no help to us. We could see what the daily temperature was in Auckland and Washington and Rome and San Francisco, but no reading for Reykjavik. It's just above the pictures they show on the weather forecast on telly every night. You can get sneak views of the weather in France and Spain when the weather forecaster moves position slightly, but no matter how you try to look past them at Iceland, there's no joy. The guidebooks weren't much better – they don't seem to expect visitors in February. So being pragmatic, and thinking that there was no point in buying things I'd never wear here, I just wore my boots and overcoat, jumper, hat, scarf and gloves, and I packed my bathing togs in my hand luggage (which is all I ever travel with).

It was just below freezing when we arrived, minus two, and it varied between that and minus six or so for the whole time, so I got it right on the clothes. The big thing about Iceland in February was not the wildlife as such, but the wonderful geological sights, which of course are to be seen all the year round. We arrived on Sunday afternoon and were to leave on Wednesday morning, so there was no time to lose. Our guide Jon met us at the airport, which is about forty kilometres west of Reykjavik, and as soon as we got into his four-wheel drive the trip was on. First stop – a swim out of doors. Just as well I had the togs.

Iceland is perched over an area of instability in the earth's crust and this causes heat to rise up under the country. This heats any water it meets on the way up and if this water is within rocks under pressure, it heats to well over the hundred degrees that we associate with boiling water. The heat from this water can be used in heat exchangers to make electricity, and some of the Icelanders' electricity is made in this way. The cooled water at the electricity plant a few kilometres outside the airport is just poured away after use, back into the ground from whence it came, at a much cooler temperature of course, say only forty degrees. But over the last twenty years or so, instead of it all disappearing down cracks in the rocks, the impurities in the water have filled all the spaces and a lake has formed. This lake is pure white because the minerals that are precipitating out of the water give it this colour, and it sits among the blackest rocks imaginable, so that the whole effect is of a steaming lake of milk in a coal shed. Presumably it reflects the blue sky at times, as the whole area is called the Blue Lagoon.

Before you could turn round, there we were in a lovely changing room divesting ourselves of all our woollies and donning the togs for a dip. I assumed that there would be a heated tunnel leading from the changing rooms to the water's edge – but nah. You opened the door, walked outside in your togs and bare feet (being careful not to slip on the ice) and got into that lagoon in record-breaking time. And it was lovely – like the nicest bath you ever had.

And it never got cold like a bath would. Getting out, of course, was not anticipated at all, and we made the first bit of the radio programme up to our necks in hot water – literally. But eventually it got dark and Jon wanted to get to Reykjavik, so once more a streak from the water across the icy ground to the hot showers and changing rooms.

On Monday we went to see the tourist sights – the Great Geysir (that is how it is spelt, and from that name comes our word 'geyser'), the beautiful Gullfoss waterfall and the part of Iceland where the American and European plates are parting company. Derek made a *faux pas* at breakfast and sleepily took an egg which he assumed was hard-boiled, only to discover after he had cracked it open on his plate that it was from a section of the buffet where breakfasters could cook their eggs to their liking. So this gave him the idea of taking another raw one with him to the Geysir to see if the water there was really as hot as all that. Would it be hot enough to boil an egg?

The Geysir was spouting merrily as we arrived. The superheated water was forced to the surface through a very narrow crack and, as the pressure on it was suddenly released as it emerged, it changed with a whoosh to a column of superheated steam maybe ten metres high. It made very satisfactory noises for radio, so we stood close by and 'interviewed' it several times. All around were bigger holes where there was no pressure on the water, so it reached the surface merely heated to boiling as opposed to being superheated and exploding as steam. One of these would be ideal to boil the egg. We could hardly drop it in, because we would have to retrieve it after four minutes. Our guide was amazed at such proceedings. Any other tourists he had ever guided here just looked, took photos and went away. We were mad, he said. We were too. A spare pair of socks was commandeered and I was volunteered to hold the egg over the boiling hole for four minutes. The hole didn't turn out to be a geyser, and I survived the experience. Let no one say I cannot boil an egg. It was perfectly cooked – white firm, yolk just runny. I didn't even get to eat it after all that – Derek and Jon polished it off between them.

On to Gulfoss, a waterfall which is frozen at this time of year, situated on a fast-flowing river, which emerges from one of the glaciers that covers so much of central Iceland. While there wasn't much snow on the ground, it was freezing hard and we saw no wildlife at all on the way there. There were Icelandic ponies to be seen, though, and lots of them. Apparently all farming was done with these animals until about twenty years ago, and the farmers couldn't bear to part with them. So they roam free in a desolate countryside with no fields, no grass, no hedges, and the farmers put out fodder drops for them, to tide them over the winter. The waterfall was magnificent – a sheet of gleaming white ice with the sun bouncing a rainbow off it, and in the distance we could see the glacier from whence it came. Ireland it was not.

On then to this great divide separating America from Europe, where the magma that comes up from the central

Atlantic ridge hardens to form Iceland. It then begins to split in two separate directions, one lot heading west and the other side heading east. These phenomena occur only as fast as your fingernails grow, so we were not really in danger of the ground opening up and swallowing us. It didn't even make satisfactory creaky noises for the microphone and it got colder and colder as we stood there drawing word pictures for the folks back home. Enough of this! Back to Reykjavik for our feast, which Jon had assured us was going to be something else again.

People have lived in this country since the seventh century and they have devised ways of surviving the winter when no food could be grown. Freeze it, you might think, sure isn't the place called Iceland. But no, it's not reliably cold enough – it isn't Greenland, where you can rely on the deep-freeze effect all winter. Here, because of troughs of low pressure and high pressure and prevailing westerly winds, you cannot rely on it to stay cold enough all the time to keep food frozen all winter. So they smoke and salt things as people do in other northern countries, but their salted meat is made from lamb, rather than the ham or corned beef we are used to, and it was a new one on me. It tasted like ham when you first chewed it and then halfway through eating it turned to lamb in your mouth. Most amazing.

Actually, our meal was to be a mixture of two feasts. One was to celebrate the start of Lent, when salted lamb, dried peas and spuds constituted the traditional Shrove meal, and it was grand. The other feast really had taken place the week before and we were given just a sample of it, as we were not there at the right time. Just as well, really, since this earlier feast was to polish off all the food that had been kept over the winter, now that spring was here and they would no longer need it. Lamb and mutton is their main meat, since the land doesn't grow enough grass to support cows. As well as salting the lamb, they steep it in a sort of fermented yoghurt which has the effect of pickling it. They waste no part of the beast – the pickled testicles are served separately. They make haggis-type sausages from the sheep's stomach and dry these out so that they will survive. But this is the *pièce de résistance* – they actually use the winter period to make something edible that otherwise they couldn't eat: shark. The Greenland shark to be precise. Other species of shark are perfectly edible, and you see steaks of it on sale on supermarket fish counters, even in conservative old Ireland. But the Greenland shark is a huge creature, which was hunted by Icelanders for its liver, which could contain up to three barrels of oil. Its skin was fairly useful as well, because it was so tough it could be used for making boots and shoes. But the flesh contains cyanic acid and eating it would cause death from cyanide poisoning.

However, it was discovered (how *are* these things discovered?) that if the mountain of flesh was buried, it fermented and the acid leached out of it and it would then be safe to eat. So shark caught for oil and boots at the start of winter were then buried and, by the end of the winter, they were safe to eat. So pieces of this rotten shark were the high spot of the winter feast we were given, which also included the pickled sheeps' testicles, the haggis, the salted lamb and a small shot glass of clear liquid to wash it down. The smell was very strong and not particularly inviting. In fact, it smelt like a piece of Camembert you might find at the bottom of the fridge after being away for a month. The Icelanders stood around and kindly explained everything in perfect English. We started with the lamb and worked up to the shark, for which we were advised to keep our drink. And it did taste pretty bad. You couldn't imagine anyone looking forward to digging some up for the dinner. We gulped the drink, a burning aquavit called Black Death. Did it cure or cause the black death? I wonder. You'd want to be on your last gasp of hunger to want to eat the rotten shark – the *hakarl* – either that or be making a radio programme.

Reykjavik itself has the look of a frontier town. There is no timber in Iceland. Much less than 1 per cent of it is forested, and early settlers cut down what there was for fuel. The houses in the city are made from cement and local materials. The roofs are of corrugated galvanised steel, such as we are familiar with here on outbuildings, and are painted brightly. The lake in front of the town hall that day in February was full of Whooper swans. Whooper swans in Ireland are wild and hard to see, but these ones were coming up to be hand-fed with pieces of bread like the ducks in St Stephen's Green in Dublin.

And was it fierce expensive? Well, it depends on what you're buying I suppose. Houses were cheaper than here, petrol just about the same or a little dearer. Lamb and fish in the supermarkets were about half the price they are here. Eating out and drinking out, what visitors do, was about twice the price it is here – which is saying something. Drink used to be prohibited, because people drank too much and lost the run of themselves, and beer has only been available on sale in the last twenty years. Wine at dinner in a restaurant seemed to start at about €40 for the cheapest plonk – wine that we could buy here in an off-licence for €5 and probably cost less than the cork and the bottle in the country of origin. Then again, things that you'd think would be ruinously expensive because of having to be imported, such as cut flowers, tomatoes, peppers, bananas, were surprisingly inexpensive, because it turns out they grow them there all the year round. No, I didn't have an overdose of Black Death – the fact is that greenhouses are common, heated by hot water which comes free from the ground and lit during the long dark winter by banks of light powered by cheap, renewable electricity from water both heated and flowing.

You always have to leave something to go back for. We'll have to go back to see the Northern Lights. The postcards on display were full of beautiful night skies suffused with crimson, emerald, acid yellow, but we saw none of them, even though we nearly froze gazing at the sky. They happen all the year there, we were assured, though not, of course, every night and not the three nights we were there. They happen in summer too, but the sky is too bright to see

them. So the *Aurora Borealis*, which conjured up such images in our minds when we learnt the words in school, are still on the to-do list. Still, they probably wouldn't have made good radio anyway!

THINGS THAT SPARKLE IN THE **NIGHT**

JUST AS DIFFERENT THINGS come out in the garden at night when the birds have gone to bed, so too a whole different collection of animals emerges underwater when it becomes dark. Night-diving to see these is something else. When I say dark, it really is dark down there in the sea at night. There is no ambient light from streetlights, no reflection from the sky; such weak light cannot penetrate down into the water. You are totally dependent on what you can see by the light of your torch. All around is a wall of darkness. Doesn't do to think too much about what might be out there lurking just beyond the reach of the torch.

I always thought that night divers were mad. It's scary

enough going down during the day, when at least you can see and know which way is down and which up. At night the space seems much more enclosed. You really are dependent on the quality of your diving gear and on the length of time the torch batteries will last underwater. But the lure of the completely different selection of wildlife (and the fact that my buddy promised to hold my hand the whole time) was stronger than my perfectly reasonable fears, and so it was that I found myself one dark night at the back of the car changing into my wetsuit and checking and double-checking the gear – contents gauge, life jacket, torch and batteries, reserve valves, regulator, knife, gloves. In the end, I could delay no longer, and off we went to the end of the pier to jump in.

And, first surprise, as we gazed down towards the inky waters, it wasn't all dark down there. Once anything hit the water, a shower of sparks seemed to appear. There seemed to be tiny points of light in the water that only appeared when it was disturbed and they were moved suddenly. These lights are in fact a kind of phosphorescent plankton called dinoflagellates, which glow with a cold light when suddenly disturbed. By dropping in stones from the pier, we could cause a shower of sparks to occur where the stones hit the water. The species in our waters is called *Noctiluca* – a nightlight in other words. They are much more common in warmer waters, where the wake of a passing ship can consist of a twinkling path in the water. Amazingly in this day and age, not a great deal is known about how this light is actually produced. The wonderfully named substance luciferin is involved. This does not, sadly, mean direct interference from the lower regions of the next world. The fact that Lucifer was the name of one of the four archangels who occupied the highest levels of heaven above the cherubim and the seraphim, and who subsequently was expelled for the sin of pride, means that the name is forever associated with hell. But Latin scholars will know, of course, that the word merely means light carrier, and this is precisely what the luciferin in the *Noctiluca* does. When an enzyme in the cells of an organism that contains luciferin is oxidised, light is produced. Why, is another matter. Why would a big shoal of these tiny creatures draw attention to themselves in this way when disturbed? Surely they would provide a tasty mouthful for filter feeders higher up on the food chain, who would be attracted to their presence by the lights? But study of evolution tells us that there must be something in it for the species itself or it would have caused its extinction long ago.

We cannot ponder evolution any longer. Are you getting in or not? And so we carefully descend the steps, and get in very gently – no flamboyant leaping backwards off the edge here. The cold of the water as it fills the wetsuit is somehow reassuring in its unwelcome familiarity. And then down we go. The dive will involve swimming along the bottom just above the rocks out off the coast to a depth of thirty feet or so, and watching the night-time scene. And there is plenty to see. There seems to be an endless amount of crabs scurrying over the bottom, much more so than during the day. We are on the lookout for more exotic creatures – lobsters. These live in rocky crevices and defend the entrances to them with their large claws. During the daytime, if you were to spot a claw waving from a hole in the rock, any investigation would cause it to be drawn in sharpish. The holes are always bigger than the lobsters and they retreat at the slightest interference. But they are hunters, not filter feeders. So they must come out to find food, and this they do under the cover of darkness. It is truly an amazing sight to see a large, dark purple lobster walking backwards along the seabed. They can only go backwards, but they can certainly move with strong contractions of their tails when disturbed.

They are out looking for food, and like the crabs they are scavengers. They will eat dead food, and so play their role in tidying up the seabed by mopping up any dead or dying creatures they come across. Fishermen are using this knowledge when they bait and sink lobster pots to catch them. The bait, lumps of mackerel or other fish, can be smelt from a distance and the lobster soon arrives, walking backwards. It reverses in through the opening in the pot and soon demolishes the tasty bait. But, alas, it can't turn around in the pot to reverse out the way it came, and it can't move forward, so there it must remain until the pot is lifted. It is not injured or hurt in any way, just trapped. Crabs come into the pot as well, for they too are partial to pieces of dead fish, and by the time the fisherman comes to lift the pot, the crabs may be so numerous that they are fighting among themselves.

The lobsters are never too numerous any more, however, and there are strict measures in place to ensure that the species is not fished out. Lobsters can live to a great age and reach very large sizes. You'd never think this looking at the paltry specimens in restaurant tanks with rubber bands around their claws. Restaurants, obsessed with portion size, have created a demand for one-man dinners, and these are at the very lowest edge of sustainability. If you catch lobsters that are so small that they have not bred even once, how is the species to survive? Research on lobsters is being carried out around Irish waters to determine how fast our lobsters grow and when they breed. Such guinea-pig lobsters have notches cut into the shell of their tails and woe betide any fisherman or restaurant owner found with one in their possession. As well as that, there is a minimum size for legally caught lobsters, and the fishermen all have a slide-rule job on board to measure the lobster as they remove it from the pot. Too small and it must go over the side to live another day and to breed. But when you see a very large lobster walking along on the seabed in the light of the torch it really is a worthy foe to be admired. There is nothing noble about a manacled wee lobster (even if is the minimum size) languishing in the bottom of a restaurant tank waiting for customers with more money than sense. Crabs are much tastier in my opinion.

We could have gone right up to the rocks to see if there

were any lobsters just emerging, but lobsters aren't the only creatures that live in holes in rocks. Conger eels live there too and they have a fearsome reputation. Everybody knows that they bite the fingers clean off fishermen who have to disentangle them from catches. While they probably wouldn't come out and grab you if you swam too close, you wouldn't be on for poking your hand into holes, certainly not in the dead of night, gloves or no gloves. They do come out of the holes and swim around close to their rocky homes, looking for food at night. They are substantial creatures and can grow up to ten feet long. They eat crabs, fish and even octopus, itself a creature that is no pushover. They feature in Mediterranean fish catches and are an essential component of the beautiful seafood soup, *bouillabaisse*. The Welsh, the Portuguese, the Spaniards, the French and the Cornish people all have recipes for it, but there are no traditional Irish recipes. Maybe the Irish were wise in leaving well enough alone.

Slowly onwards, holding hands, with two torches searching the seabed. More movement. Sort of a whoosh really. What is it? Close investigation seems to reveal brownish hollow tubes the size of pencils all just standing in a row. But then my buddy, who has been down before, points slowly, and beyond the pencils we can see another stand of tubes, but this time they have long fronds sticking out of the top of them waving gently in the water – fan worms. These are filter feeders that live in strong tubes and when the coast is clear they stick up their heads above the parapet and wave their long colourful food-catching gills in the water. They definitely have a head designed for the job. They carry these flower-like gills on their eyes, of which they have many, and the gills are in a circle like a crown surrounding their mouth. Waving these gills in the water allows them to extract oxygen and chases any small prey into the centre of the crown, where the mouth is open and waiting. They'd be a tasty mouthful themselves for a hungry crab, so at the slightest water disturbance they whoosh themselves back down into their tube and out of danger. You have to be really lucky and careful to see them.

I knew that there'd be loads of snails down there – after all, what are periwinkles and limpets and topshells only snails in the sea? The shell protects them from damage by the waves and we have no compunction about eating winkles – they don't seem to be the same, somehow, as *escargots*. But I hadn't known that slugs have made the bottom of the sea their own as well. They have. There is a whole branch of sea creatures called sea slugs and we were just about to see one. We were coming back in now and had reached the seaweeds again, which indicate very shallow water, when we espied a brownish blob swimming just above the seaweed. By day you'd never notice such a thing, but the world you can see is so reduced at night that you pay attention to everything. This creature was a sea hare and it had four horns sticking up out of the front of its head, just like a land slug. Of course we could not resist poking it with our fingers – after all, what could a slug do to you? – and we were quite taken aback to see it issue a large purple cloud of liquid out of itself. Surely we hadn't injured it? – we only gave it a little poke. How could it be so sensitive? When the cloud cleared, it was gone. We had fallen for the oldest magician's trick – distraction. While we were staring at the purple cloud, the slug, not called the sea hare for nothing, had smartly departed in the opposite direction and was now safely camouflaged among the seaweeds.

Time to come up. We rose slowly, slower than our bubbles, with the torches shining on the bubbles. As we neared the surface, we could see that we had risen among a shoal of sea gooseberries. These were not the unwanted partners at some sea dance, but completely transparent balls of jelly about the size of gooseberries. Because they had long tentacles hanging out of them, I feared that they were some sort of jellyfish. But I soon realised that I was not getting stung, although they were swimming past my face. These are small carnivores that really should be called sea cowboys, as they use their tentacles as lassoes, catching tiny prey and putting them into their mouths. I bet they were attracted by the bio-luminescence of the *Noctiluca*, who were now, of course, hiding their lights under bushels, as none could be seen, and the gooseberries were dining on light-free fare.

This luminescence is not just confined to surface creatures. Apparently it plays a big role in the lives of creatures who live in exterior darkness – the regions of the ocean below a thousand metres, where light never reaches. Bacteria produce the glow, and fish and other creatures carry pockets of these glowing bacteria around on their skin like tattoos. There are all sorts of arrangements. Some just carry the light permanently as stripes on their skin. Others have fierce complicated arrangements altogether and can cover the glowing area with skin, or rotate it so that the light is suddenly switched off. There is even a deep-sea squid whose camouflage cloud is not made of the purple ink we are familiar with in our calamari, but which can produce a luminous cloud when disturbed. It must be like the Milky Way at those depths. Imagine extracting that to make a sauce for your pasta! It would glow in the dark. Mind you, even our regular shallow-water squid can shine in the dark when freshly caught. They would have the luminous bacteria in the slime of their skin. But to catch them at it, you'd have to have unwashed and very fresh squid in your fridge, you'd have to make sure the internal light bulb was not working and you'd have to open it at night when the kitchen is dark. It would be enough to put you right off raiding the fridge for a midnight snack if you encountered a glow-in-the-dark squid. But truly you cannot blame Sellafield for this one.

There are theories why this luminescence is so common in the very dark ocean, where up to two-thirds of the resident species exhibit this phenomenon. It could be a lure to attract curious onlookers. Certainly some fish have the luminosity on their barbels or tentacles. Curious gawkers are quickly snapped up by hungry jaws. Or it could be a communication system – yoo-hoo, I'm over here! (It must be very hard to find a mate if you live in perpetual darkness.) Then there are the crafty lot who can turn off the light. They lure food near, then turn off the light and pounce in the darkness. Or it may be a signal that this is my territory, enter at your peril. Or indeed it could be like the red warning colour on the ladybirds, a sign that the wearer tastes horrible. Or it might just be – although this is just too simple for words – the creature's flashlight: maybe it uses the light to see where it is going and what is going on all round it. It is probably all of these things and a few more we haven't thought of besides.

Certainly, after a night dive, you are very sceptical about the theory that humans spent some time in their evolutionary past living in water. We can't see there at night, we can't smell anything in the water (sharks can smell one part of blood per million), we look like injured fish as we flap our ungainly fins, we cannot use the one sense the others don't have – our speech – and we cannot even stay down there all that long even with an aqua lung. But diving at night is the business if you want a buzz. The fact that you survive the dive at all – never mind all the creatures that you see, and the even more fearsome ones that are surely there too – is thrilling. I certainly came away with a different point of view. But I didn't pursue a career as a night-dive leader!

DECONSTRUCTING THE TALE OF THE SALMON OF KNOWLEDGE

THE SALMON OF KNOWLEDGE is the fish of legends. He featured on the old two-shilling piece and was promoted to the ten pence piece after the money changed to the decimal system. He was the source of the wisdom of Fionn Mac Cumhaill, the leader of the Fianna. There's not a schoolchild going but knows the tale. But if he was such a smart fish, how come he got caught in the first place? The tale does not stand up to close scrutiny.

At the beginning of this story, we are introduced to the salmon, who lived in the river Boyne in County Meath. He got his wisdom by eating the nuts of the nine hazel trees that grew around the sacred pool at the source of the Boyne. So it was the hazel trees that had the wisdom really. They still have, as any dowser who uses a forked hazel bough to divine water will tell you. The druids at the time were well aware of the magical qualities of hazelnuts and indeed of the concentrating ability of the food chain. The salmon that ate the nuts gained all the wisdom, and the man who ate the salmon would in turn be the wisest man in Ireland. So the men spent their time on the banks of the Boyne trying to catch the Salmon of Knowledge. If it was so partial to magic hazelnuts, why didn't they use those as bait? (Maybe they did.) Eventually, one of their number, Finnéagas, managed to catch the salmon and recognised it for what it was – a potential source of all knowledge and wisdom. If you or I caught such a thing, do you think we'd let it out of our hands? We'd probably take a bite of it raw, sushi style, in order to get the knowledge immediately. But what did the druid, who is described as a scholar and a poet, do? He entrusted the fish and the cooking of it to a pimply teenage youth called Fionn Mac Cumhaill whom he was minding since his father was killed, told him to cook it carefully and not eat any of it and then *went away* and left the fish that he had been trying all his life to catch. No wonder the powers that be determined that he didn't deserve to get all this wisdom. A few street smarts instead of all this poetry would have been more useful. He wandered back when he felt the salmon should be done, having left all the collecting of the kindling and the making of the fire and the peeling of the willow branch for a roasting spit and the gutting of the fish and the turning of the cooking fish on the spit to the person at home slaving over the hot fire, like many a man no doubt. And I am not a bit sorry for him that he got his comeuppance. Fionn, being a resourceful lad, and no doubt now full of wisdom, had an excuse for his changed appearance when Finnéagas came home and spoke to him. He had merely pressed a burning blister on the skin's surface with his bare thumb (what was he like?) and, of course, oven gloves not having been invented yet, burnt it. A piece of burning salmon skin stuck to his thumb – well it would, wouldn't it? – and Fionn inadvertently ate it as he sucked his burnt digit. They were both lucky some marauding gull hadn't landed on the fish guts and eaten them first. Ever afterwards, the wisdom was concentrated in Fionn's thumb and he had to suck it every time he wanted to know anything.

We don't hear anything more about Finnéagas after this. Did he become vegetarian and concentrate on the nuts of the hazel tree? What good did all the knowledge do Fionn? Did it last him all his life? Why didn't it tell him not to be such a dirty old man pursuing poor Diarmuid and Gráinne all around Ireland in his later years? It might dawn on a man with no wisdom at all that a young one might prefer the young handsome Diarmuid to an auld fella like himself. Not so the deluded Fionn Mac Cumhaill. Maybe Finnéagas was better off without the gift of wisdom after all.

But what about the salmon? Well, salmon have always

been associated with Irish rivers. So abundant were they in the old days that the labourers working on the building of the monastery in Graiguenamanagh had it written into their contract of employment that they should not be given salmon for their dinner any more than three times a week. We cannot imagine eating wild Irish river salmon in Ireland above three times a year now, never mind three times a week. What has changed and why?

The salmon has an interesting life cycle. It spends some of its time in fresh water rivers in Ireland and some of its time in the deep Atlantic Ocean. It is born in Irish rivers. Mum and Dad, who have been hanging around for some time, finally decide one wet dark December night that the time is right. Both are full of roe. Mum excavates a shallow nest – a redd – in the gravel bed of the river, well upstream. Dad is keeping an eye on proceedings, he discourages all other rivals and swims up alongside her when the time is right. His comforting presence encourages her to discharge all her eggs into the gravel bed she has just excavated. As they emerge he releases his milt in a cloudy white stream and the eggs are all fertilised in moments. She puts the gravel back over them and the job is Oxo. They are on their own from now on. The river water flows over them, continuously supplying them with oxygen, and in due course – a month or two later, depending on the temperature of the water – they hatch out. They have a large yolk sac attached to their body to feed them for the first month as they make their way to the top of the gravel so energetically placed over them by their mother. The emerging creature doesn't look a bit like a fish and is known as an 'alevin'. It soon uses up the reservoir of food in its egg sac and changes its shape to look exactly like a real fish, and now it rejoices in the name of 'fry'. It is now a carnivore and will feed happily on any small shrimps or larvae it can catch. The thousands of eggs laid by the mother need a territory each to provide food in these rather barren upper stretches of river, and so the salmon fry spread out over a wide area. Even so, only the strongest can hold territory and, like any sibling, have no compunction chasing away their brothers and sisters from their supply of food. The weakest in the family cannot hack it and so cannot swim strongly enough to stay in their own territory. They get carried downstream, where their hapless plight is quickly noticed by hungry brown trout or watchful herons and – snap! – they are no more.

The successful fry on the territories grow big and strong and spend between one and three years here, depending on how fast they grow. When they pass the three-centimetre mark, they are elevated to the status of 'parr' and they continue growing under this moniker until they reach a decent length of over ten centimetres. Whenever this magic length is reached, a complete change takes place in the body of the little salmon. Puberty was never like this. First of all it changes colour from the brown camouflage jacket it has been wearing since its egg-yolk days and it acquires a beautiful silver coat. It also feels a great desire to swim downstream, something that was only for losers a few short months ago. In fact the fish is responding to the call of the sea; it is swimming downstream purposefully to leave the river altogether to go to sea. This is a huge undertaking. The sea is much saltier than the river and if the parr went straight out into the briny it would shrivel up like a prune, as its fresh water contents rushed out through its skin in a vain attempt to establish an equilibrium. So the puberty stage must involve more than getting a new shiny coat. And it does. Changes also take place in the mechanisms of the fish's body so that it is able to deal with a salty environment. The default options are reset as it were. And so the creature, henceforth known as a 'smolt', heads off out to sea some April evening, two or three years after it was born, with the memory and the smell of where it grew up indelibly imprinted on its brain.

Where do they go? Nobody knew until recently. They just went off out into the ocean and were never encountered out there. Recent tagging studies carried out by fisheries' research officers have revealed that they swim north up the Atlantic to the Norwegian coast. They feed abundantly in the ocean and grow big and strong. About two years later, they feel homesick or broody or amorous or something, and so they leave the Norwegian coast to travel back. They can be up to two kilos in weight and – yes, you've guessed it – they have changed their name again and are now 'grilse' to all their friends. They swim back the way they came and they can recognise in the ocean the smell of their own river, their own place. Back they come into the estuary, the summer fish, on their way back home to the spot where they were born. But again they cannot dash straight in. They linger in the estuaries, becoming acclimatised anew to the fresh water and waiting for a summer flood, so that they can traverse even waterfalls in their unstoppable journey upstream. And they never feed in fresh water again. They have put on lots of condition in the ocean and this food has to last them for six months or more.

So what was the Salmon of Knowledge doing eating hazelnuts or indeed anything else? And if they don't eat, how come fishermen are out fishing for them with rods and lines? Apparently they haven't forgotten the eating habit and they make lunges at things, although they don't actually swallow them. Isn't that the pits? Just going for something out of boredom and curiosity, something you can't even eat anyway, and you get impaled on a hook.

They don't quite all get caught, however, and some will make it right back to the exact waters where they were spawned. As they swim back upriver again, their colour changes back from the sea silver to a more reddish-brown colour, which helps to camouflage them in the river waters. In the females, the eggs grow and, by the time they are ready to be laid, they will occupy the whole underside of her body, four thousand eggs each the size of a pea. The male hasn't been wasting his energy either and he is making a large quantity of milt in readiness for mating. This activity affects his jaw, and the lower one changes its shape, developing an upward-curving hook called the 'kype'. There certainly is a lot of specialised vocabulary associated with salmon.

After mating, both parents are spent completely. Most of them die, having used up all their energy swimming back up here, mating and producing eggs and milt. Some of them do make their way back down again to sea, mostly females, it must be said, and go to sea again. These experienced ladies can now be called 'kelts'. Grilse are only between two and four kilos in weight, but there are salmon that are much bigger than that in Irish rivers. These are females that don't come back with the other grilse but head across the ocean to the Greenland coast and spend several more years there putting on condition again before returning. Apparently, only females do this. The males are so anxious to get home to mate the minute they are able to, that they don't make the journey across the ocean. Much research on salmon and where they go is carried out in Borrisoshrule in County Mayo, where the researchers fertilise the eggs and rear the young salmon in controlled conditions. They then tag them with an implant and let them off. The salmon instinctively home back again to the exact spot where they were released into the river and they can be caught again, examined, aged, sexed and their eggs and milt harvested for the next generation.

Fewer and fewer of our wild salmon are making it back to their spawning beds. And indeed they may not find them in any condition to allow breeding. The gravel beds must be there, not swept away in an arterial drainage scheme. The water flowing over the fertilised eggs must be oxygen-rich. Water that has organic matter added to it, or which has received too much in the way of nitrates or phosphates won't do. And then the water in the ocean is changing temperature, with climate change, and the new temper- atures are affecting the salmon. So is salmon farming the answer? Farming food is what we have always done when hunting-gathering is no longer viable. We farm beef, poultry, pork, so fish farming is more of the same surely? Yes, but... The salmon are farmed in fish cages in sea water and fed a diet decided by the fish farmer. Salmon are carnivores, so the farmed fish have to be fed a meat diet as it were. So fish are caught and processed to feed to the salmon. It takes four pounds of processed fish to produce one pound of farmed salmon meat, hardly a sustainable conversion, seeing as it is wild small fish species that are used. Salmon swim long distances in their lives, even the ones that only go to Norway. Muscle that works produces tasty flesh. The salmon in the cages in the fish farms don't swim very far and their muscles are not much used. The proof of the pudding is in the eating. The wild salmon wins hands down. Would that we could be offered it more than three times a week! The relative availability of both sorts is reflected in the price. Farmed salmon is one of the most inexpensive fish you can buy in the fishmongers (itself a vanishing trade in Ireland), and wild salmon one of the scarcest and the dearest. Perhaps ranching is the answer. This is what they do in Borrisoshrule – fertilising the eggs and rearing the young in controlled conditions of safety and then releasing them to take their chances. Their strong homing instinct ensures they return with well-toned muscles, having eaten a diet of food they selected and caught themselves.

So where does all that leave the Salmon of Knowledge? Were we ever told what weight it was? What time of year was it caught? Was it male or female? Did Finnéagas ever eat the rest of it? But maybe I am being far too pedantic and we shouldn't spoil a good story with the facts.

THE **EXCITING LIFE** OF THE **COURTROOM** SCIENTIST

WHEN YOU ARE growing up and deciding what you want to be, anything seems possible. If you want to be an architect, you see yourself as standing up defending (successfully!) your plans for a thoroughly modern building before an oral hearing. If you want to be a train driver, it's the TGV in France or the like that you see yourself driving. If you want to be a zoologist, you picture yourself discovering animals new to science, which of course will be called after you. Unfortunately, reality rarely lives up to such expectations. But sometimes scientists do happen to be in the right place at the right time.

A customer drinking a pint of stout in a public house some time ago noticed a foreign object in the glass when he got to the end of his pint. Upon closer scrutiny, this foreign object turned out to be a slug. The customer was outraged. How come he had been served a pint of stout with a slug in it? This was not good enough. He was going to take the matter further. The glass, complete with slug, was kept as evidence, his solicitor was informed and the matter was brought to the attention of the public house. The public house determined to fight the case. They definitely had not served a pint with a slug in it and were not going to compensate the man for the fetch he had received when he saw the creature after the pint was consumed. As the man was able to complain and to engage a solicitor, he had obviously survived the experience.

The case was scheduled to appear before the district judge. The man and the solicitor had the glass with the – by now – remains of the slug in it. The public house, however, had a secret weapon – a scientist! This is why anyone would become a scientist, to investigate matters like this. Was it really a slug? If so, could it come out of a beer tap into a pint of stout and be visible at the bottom when the pint was finished? Imagine the fieldwork involved! First of all, the glass plus slug had to be officially borrowed to determine if it was really a slug that was there in the first place. That wasn't so difficult to determine. 'Afraid so, it was definitely a slug, your honour, that was in the glass.' Next question for the scientist – how could it have got there?

The pub took this case so seriously that they donated a keg of stout to the scientist for the required series of experiments. Several slugs were added to the keg of beer. It was connected to the taps and all the pints that the keg held were pulled and examined for slugs.

Unfortunately for the poor slugs, none of them survived, in anything like their entirety, the journey up through the keg and the lines and the tap and into the glass. No recognisable bits of slug could be found in any of the pints, never mind a whole one lurking at the end of the glass, post-libation. What a waste of good stout! Perhaps the slug was in the glass when the barman went to pour the pint. But the barman was completely clear on this point – he had total recall, there definitely was no slug present, the glass was totally empty and perfectly clean. Scientific fieldwork had proved that it could not have come out through the tap with the stout itself. So it could only get into the glass after the pint was poured and settled and had been handed over. If it fell from the barman, it would land on the new head on a full pint. Would it sink straight through immediately, or would the head support it, so the customer would see it if it had arrived in this way? Further research. More slugs were collected and the pints were lined up. A slug was dropped into each glass on to the new head. And in no case did the slug sink like a stone through the fresh head. It was supported there by the head of stout and would have been plainly visible to any toper as he raised his pint to his lips.

'But there was a slug at the bottom of my pint, your

honour. Everyone agrees that that is so.' The question was: how did it get in? The intrepid scientist established, with further bouts of fieldwork, that as a pint is drunk and the level gets lower in the glass, the head gets smaller and weaker. Generally, pints are not polished off in one go. Seasoned pint drinkers raise the glass, have a drink, then replace the glass on the counter or table and continue the conversation. At a certain stage in the drinking of the pint in question, the head would be reduced enough in size and strength to allow a slug through, if it fell into the glass at that precise time. This part of the research took some considerable time, as the pints had to be drunk just as they would be in a pub. Pouring away small quantities of stout every so often is not the same as drinking, and the fieldwork had to be done scientifically. So the pints were set up and drunk in a measured fashion. How many gulps, over what period of time, led to a situation where a slug would sink instantly on the remaining head? Hard work, but someone's got to do it. Finally a situation was arrived at where such a thing could happen.

Our man was adamant that he had not left his pint at any stage, so it couldn't have been contaminated by a slug-dropping passer-by. So the only possible solution was that the slug had somehow come from the drinker himself. Was this likely? Well, yes, as it happens. He worked outdoors on the land and might reasonably be expected to encounter slugs in his everyday work. If one had adhered to his arm or his sleeve, the scene was set. The judge was delighted.

'Tell me, how many slugs would you normally have out of a pint before you had it all gone?' On the balance of probability the man had inadvertently added the slug to the pint himself, just at the moment when the head could not support it and so it fell without a trace into the black depths of the half-drunk pint of stout. Gives a whole new meaning to the expression 'make a hole in that pint'. Case dismissed.

What would you have with your pint in the pub? Well, you might have a bag of crisps. Imagine the consternation of the woman eating her crisps with half an eye on the telly, when she discovered that her hand contained not only a selection of the best cheese and onion but a wriggling earwig as well. Nothing could dissuade her from the notion that the earwig was in the bag of crisps and that only for the programme on the telly was so brutal, she would have eaten it with the crisps. Mind you, if the programme had been riveting she might never have noticed. Maybe *Mooney Goes Wild* should be on the box.

Of course she was outraged and brought her complaint to the manufacturers of the crisps. And our intrepid scientist was called in once more, this time to defend the earwig, who was being accused of getting packaged with the crisps and loitering in the bag with intent to terrify decent citizenry. Was it possible? Could the earwig survive the crisp-making exercise and live in an airtight bag? Our scientist looked at the possibility. No earwig could survive the slicing of the potatoes, the heat of the oven, the salting procedures, the hygienic packing. No, it could not have emerged alive and kicking from a sealed bag of crisps, which apparently this was.

But it was there. Where could it have come from? Earwigs are well known to be thigmotaxic, which means they like being at rest in tight spaces, although not necessarily in ears, in spite of their name. So, if you scientifically examine a bag of crisps you will note that in certain sorts the bag has a fold up its backbone, as it were. And it was in this fold, outside the bag, that our earwig was having a grand rest when he was rudely disturbed by the bag being ripped open. He hastened to a darker place, which was inside the bag. His sojourn there was not long. He was soon grabbed, along with the crisps, in whose contours he had sought shelter.

So in court the scientific evidence was that a live earwig, as was found on this occasion, could not have come originally from inside a sealed crisp bag. It was worth the crisp manufacturer's while engaging the scientist as an expert witness. Case dismissed. But how did it get into the fold in the outside of the bag? And is it acceptable to sell bags of crisps complete with extra protein included on the outside? Well that was *scéal eile,* and one which our plaintiff did not pursue. I suppose look before you leap is good advice for crisp-eaters as well as earwigs.

But do the scientists always win when called to be expert witnesses? Certainly Richard Collins gave such a good account of the swan's feelings when it had not got enough sliced pan from its human feeder to lead the judge to declare that it was having a 'bad hair day' and find in its favour.

But what about our poor shopper who bought a pound of mince in the butcher's and when he came to eat it, found it covered in maggots? Of course he wished to sue the butcher. So the scientist was consulted by the defendant – the butcher – to establish what the maggots were, how long they could have been in the mince and in whose establishment the contamination could have occurred. So the scientist worked on the case. Maggots are the young of bluebottles. A female bluebottle would have to lay the eggs on unprotected meat. Where could this have happened? Eggs are tiny and not easily seen. They hatch out quickly in heat, but not in cold. They smartly grow to white maggot proportions on such lovely food if the temperature is right. Did the butcher have the meat in protected cold storage? Did the customer leave the messages hanging about? Could the fly have gained access while the meat was in his possession? How long after buying it did the purchaser decide to eat it? How quickly does the lifecycle of a bluebottle occur in the heat of the summer? How long elapses between eggs being laid and maggots appearing? Our scientist was in full pursuit of all the facts when the case was called. It was known in advance who the judge was going to be. And – consternation! – it was a man who liked his beef. He was partial to a good steak. He would not like to hear of a man with maggots in his mince. He would surely empathise with such a trauma. Better not risk it. The

case was settled on the steps of the courthouse. If the judge was known to be a vegetarian, I wonder what the outcome would have been.

And to think that some people imagine that scientists are serious nerds looking down microscopes all day. There should be waiting lists to get into college to study science!

NOT SAILING TO AUSTRALIA

I USED TO BE A MEMBER of the Irish Sub-Aqua Club, and a great coup of that club was their discovery of the wreck of the John Tayleur off the nose of Lambay Island. This wreck was discovered before I joined the club in 1976, but it was a favourite dive site all during my time there. The John Tayleur was a sailing ship that set out for Australia from Liverpool in 1853. It carried on board survivors of the Irish famine, among others, who were sailing to Australia with all their worldly goods, to start up a new life there. They took all their possessions with them – the women had gold coins sewn into their long skirts for security. They even brought gravestones with them, so that those who died in

Australia would not go unremembered. It was a modern sailing ship at the time, with a new iron hull, instead of the more old-fashioned wooden hulls of earlier ships.

It left Liverpool under full sail, but quickly sailed into bad weather. Gales drove them off course and the captain wasn't too sure where exactly they were. Reading the compass, he calculated they were well down the Irish Sea and away from any dangerous land. But he hadn't reckoned with the fact that the steel hull was deflecting the needle of the compass, giving a false reading, and the mist and rain parted just in time for him to see that he was running before the wind, hard aground onto the rocks off the nose of Lambay Island, just north of Dublin Bay. The ship struck with great force and was held fast on the rocks.

The sailors were an ill-trained crew. Many of them had little experience at sea and their first reaction was to clamber up the riggings on to land and run away. Women and children first, how are you – this wasn't the *Titanic*! As it turned out, that was the only way to escape. The ship broke up very slowly and there was time for more orderly passengers to climb ashore and rig up a line from the rigging to land to help the others ashore. But the women on board couldn't climb up the rigging with their heavy, wet long skirts and they certainly weren't taking them off – not with their life savings sewn into them. The ship couldn't wait. It slipped away beneath the waves, bearing every woman on board to a watery grave, with the sole exception of the captain's wife. Many of the menfolk died too, but none of the crew. What an end to the poor souls who had survived a horrible famine and hoped for a new life.

Over a hundred years later, when we dived down to see the wreck, we got no impression of a ship lying beneath the waves on its side. It looked like a timber yard, a collection of boards and planks in a great heap on the bottom. As you swam alongside underwater, you could never see the whole wreck at the same time – visibility didn't permit it. But you could look though gaps in the planks and see the cargo of tombstones still there, marking the place of death, but with no names written on them.

In fact the whole place emanated an aura of something wrong. The water seemed colder here than anywhere else. The timbers had been down there for so long that they were colonised by a fauna of their own. One particularly common sight was a coral-like growth called, fittingly enough, dead man's fingers. This is a growth of soft coral which forms on surfaces and branches in strands the size of fingers. Each finger has tentacles on it, and these wave around in the water filtering out food from the sea water. They look dead white or pale yellow to the diver's eyes and, if touched, they retract their tentacles as if they were drawing back from the touch. Eerie enough sort of behaviour from underwater life.

Even the crabs down there seem a different colour, much pinker, sort of a rusty red. It would make you wonder what they have been eating, although reason dictates that any dead body still in the wreck would have decomposed completely long since. Swimming around the wreck, looking at the sand below, mementoes of the cargo can be found. A piece of blue willow-patterned delph, the handle of a walking cane – all destined for Australia – never got further than here. Many artefacts from the ship were salvaged and are on display in the Dublin Municipal Museum, items such as the portholes and the ship's binnacle.

Coming back up to the sunlight and the warmer surface waters is welcome after such a dive, although you would want to be careful addressing remarks to your fellow diver whom you happen to spot on the surface. That black head in a rubber wetsuit with its back to you might not be what it seems. Seals breed off Lambay Island and are common in the surrounding waters. They are curious creatures and are not beyond coming along to see what is going on in their territory. Being mammals, they have to come up for a breath from time to time, so a black head breaking water near to where you are may not be a fellow-diver at all, but a curious seal. There are no records of seals ever interfering with divers – they are so much more obviously at home in the water than a diver is with a big heavy bottle – but discretion is usually the better part of valour and the field is left to the seals.

We have two species of seals off our waters, the grey seal and the much less frequently encountered 'common' seal. They are part of populations of seals that breed off the Irish and Scottish coasts, so this whole area is their territory. They come ashore to give birth and while they are at it they mate again for the next season – getting the two jobs done, as it were, for the price of one. Common seals give birth in June. They haul up on to the shore in secluded coastal spots and give birth to large pups about an eighth the size of their mother's weight. If we were to do the same, our babies would weigh over a stone at birth. They feed them for about a month on very rich milk, with up to 60 per cent fat. Then they seem to lose interest and are more concerned with queuing up for the attentions of the bull, who has the whole harem to attend to. After this they depart to sea, leaving the baby to fend for itself. The poor baby takes about two weeks to realise that Mammy is not coming back and that it will have to go fishing itself. Fortunately, it is so big and fat it can survive for two weeks until it cops on how to catch food for itself.

The story is the same for the grey seal. They haul out to have their pups around the end of September. They use the same breeding grounds each year and the adult female likes to give birth in the exact spot she used the previous year. So woe betide any new mother who happens to have plonked down here. She is sent off in no uncertain terms by the experienced mum. In fact, these maternity wards can be places of great turmoil and fighting. The males know that the mating time has come when the females are coming ashore to give birth. And while mating won't actually happen until the pups are weaned some weeks later, that doesn't deter the randy males from getting into pole position, as it were. They come ashore as well and try to make sure they are in the best place to meet the women. This may involve lying on the stretch of sand between the sea and the maternity unit. Indeed, if the stretch of sand is narrow and the mammies need all of it, they'll hang around in the shallow waters. And they occupy themselves as they wait by fighting with each other. They can inflict nasty wounds on each other's neck and flippers. There is no fair sharing out – the strongest males occupy the best vantage sites and try to mate with as many females as possible. They do not leave their hard-won territory at all, not even to feed, so they could be there for up to eight weeks without food. Isn't lust a wonderful sustenance supplier all the same! The females leave as soon as they have mated, but the males hang on until the end – they may have waited ten years for this stage of their lives and they are going to get the very last out of it. Then off they go to sea and don't come ashore again until the same time next year.

Seals are very popular with the general public. Perhaps it is because they have an appealing face. Perhaps it is because they shed tears if their eyes are too long out of salt water. Perhaps it is because of the tales that they contain the souls of people drowned at sea. Whatever the reason, people who find what they believe to be an abandoned baby seal are always very anxious that it should be rescued, and that is exactly what the Seal Sanctuary in north County Dublin does. Here the seals are cared for and nursed back to health and sometimes the seal has been released back to sea amid a welter of media coverage. We have begun the season of *Mooney Goes Wild* on more than one occasion with a seal release.

These releases are well-flagged beforehand and, on the day it is due to occur, a cast of thousands assembles on the appointed beach. I remember one such day in County Wexford, when, emboldened with the success of previous releases on the radio, it was decided to release one which would be covered by a simultaneous television and radio link. Was there ever such weather? The release was to happen live on both media at 10.45 in the morning, and precisely as the introductory music was rolling, an immense black cloud rolled in from the Saltees, darkening the sky, and the rain and wind drenched everyone. But the show went on. The seal emerged from its box, smelt the sea and made a beeline straight down the shore and into the water.

They don't always perform as well as that, as we were to learn the following year in Balbriggan in north County Dublin. There were two seals to be released this time, and the cast of thousands was augmented by local dignitaries. Keeping the crowd well back, the first was released and went straight down to the sea and practically waved at the cameras. All the VIPs got to speak on air and welcome this auspicious occasion. So the programme for the viewers at home was grand. However, after we went off air, the second seal was released. The crowds did not stand back so well this time – sure, wasn't the fuss at the first release unnecessary really! So when the second seal emerged, it got confused and, instead of heading for the sea, it made a rush at the crowd, and for a moment it looked as if it might bite the mayor on the leg. Where are the television cameras when you need them? This gave a great deal of amusement to the beholders who had remained at a safe distance. Eventually the second seal was rounded up and encouraged into the sea. A yellow mark had been placed on the seal's head to facilitate tracking it until its next moult, at which time the mark would disappear.

Fishermen aren't too fond of seals, though. They see them as rivals for scarce fish resources. And what really annoys the fishermen is the habit some seals have of taking a bite out of each fish it comes across impaled in a net by the gills. If they just took one away and ate it that would be bad enough, but to destroy a whole netful seems unforgivable. Of course, the seal is just acting on instinct. For thousands of years when seals encountered a lot of fish together, they worked as fast as they could, knowing that the shoal would quickly swim away and they'd be lucky to catch enough for a meal. How are they to know that this is not a loose shoal in the open sea, but one that is entrapped in a net? They are simply acting on instinct, trying to get as much food as possible. However, knowing why they do it doesn't make life any easier for the fishermen.

The seal releases do a lot for public awareness of wildlife and so have their educational value, but neither the grey seal nor the common seal are species which are in actual danger of extinction in our waters.

SEX, DRUGS AND ROCK'N'ROLL IN THE DARK GARDEN

DID YOU EVER WONDER what goes on out in the garden when you are all nicely tucked up asleep in bed? Among the wildlife that is! While we are creatures of the day and feel tired and sleepy when night comes, there is a complete world of wildlife that only becomes active when it gets dark. There are many reasons for this – some of them so compelling that you'd wonder why anything comes out at all during the day. One reason is that it is much cooler and damper at night, so if you feel you might suffer from dehydration, then you avoid the sunshine and heat and emerge when such threats have passed. Sharp-eyed birds are about in abundance during the daytime, so if you'd make a tasty meal for a thrush or a blackbird, then best stay under cover until they have all gone to bed. So it is no wonder that when we ourselves venture out into the garden at night and wander among the vegetables and herbaceous borders, it isn't long before we become aware of the abundance of snails and slugs that are there.

In fact, you may even hear them before you shine your torch on them, munching away at your pet hostas or prized basil plants. Snails and slugs, both members of the same group – the molluscs – have the most remarkable tongues. This structure rejoices in the name of 'radula' and is attached, if you could imagine such a thing, to the underside of the oesophagus. It is covered in rows of minute teeth, so that when the snail is eating a leaf, it rubs its tongue over and back, for all the world like a nail file – and the rasping sound is quite audible on a clear, still night. It never wears out or gets blunt either; the radula continues to grow during the creature's lifetime, with new teeth being formed on the growing bit. So you couldn't even begin to hope that old snails would have worn out their tongues eating and would thus be less efficient.

Indeed, the whole design of its body is most remarkable. Our blood is red, because it contains haemoglobin, formed from iron, to bind the oxygen. The blood of snails and slugs contains haemocyanin, a copper compound which binds the oxygen, but their blood is colourless. I wonder why it isn't the bright green shade copper becomes when it is exposed to the air – like the dome of Rathmines church in Dublin?

Their eyes are another interesting phenomenon. In fact, they could be a role model for teachers, for their eyes are out on stalks at the front of their bodies and they can use each one completely independently. If teachers had eyes like this, they could look at the blackboard with one eye and keep an eye on the class behind at exactly the same time. Snails and slugs actually have four horns, or tentacles to give them their proper title, at the front of their bodies – two long ones with the eyes at the end and two short ones. The short tentacles are what they feel and smell with, so really you could say their nostrils are out on stalks as well.

So far so weird, but it is in the reproductive department that the seriously bizarre bits are. For a start, your average common-or-garden snail is neither male nor female but both at the same time – in other words, they are hermaphrodites. But this does not in any way spoil their reproductive pleasures. They cannot mate with themselves, in spite of having all the necessary reproductive equipment, but must seek out another of the same species if they are thinking of starting a family. No problem there: on any given dark, damp, warmish night the garden is full of them. So they slither about rasping away at the lettuce leaves and keeping a stalked eye or two out for another equally minded individual. Having encountered just such a body, they snuggle up together in a slimy embrace. Their genital opening is just below their head, and both their male and female parts terminate in this one opening. Thrilling enough, you might think, but the anatomical arrangements don't stop at that. Snails and slugs have a third department to enhance their love lives even further. This is a special dart sac in the oviduct, and in here they manufacture a thin, sharp, pointed structure known as a love dart. (Honestly, I am not making this up.) During mating, they lie side by side in the required position. They each thrust a love dart into the other, apparently as stimulation, and they then exchange sperm. This makes its way up the opening into the female bit, and the eggs are subsequently formed and fertilised.

Later – several weeks later, and under much less exciting circumstances – the eggs are laid in the soil and covered with earth. The snail crawls away and never sees its eggs again. So, in spite of belonging to a one-parent family, where the parent is both the mother and the father – a perfect arrangement one might think – the offspring are homeless, abandoned orphans. But this is of no consequence. Each egg hatches out into a snail, complete with a voracious appetite, and gets to work on the garden plants that are so delicious and that the kind garden owner has so thoughtfully planted for them. Most eggs are laid in summer and autumn, and baby snails and slugs hatch out within six weeks. They take a year to reach maturity and then, all going well, they have been known to live for ten years or even longer. They hibernate each winter, sealing up the opening in their shells to keep out the cold and to prevent them from drying out.

Slugs belong to the same group as snails, even though they have no shells. To compensate for this, they produce an even stickier mucus than snails do and are much less favoured by birds, who really don't want their beaks full of sticky slime, all things being equal. This slime seems to be very strong, in some slug species at any rate, who use it to carry out what must be one of the most bizarre mating rituals of all that can take place in the garden. Astute observers among the listeners to the programme have recounted experiences of watching slugs lowering them-selves from a height by their mucus and abseiling as it were, downwards, suspended by the sticky mucus. One listener went so far as to describe it as bungee jumping, but plump and stately slugs would never move with such frivolous haste. What are they at? What do you think? Making their mating process even more thrilling, that's what!

What happens typically is this. Two slugs of the great grey species meet on the ground and decide that theirs is a match made in heaven. They both then climb up a tree – the same tree – and out on to a branch. They then each begin to lower themselves off the branch into the air below, suspended only by a rope of sticky mucus. They lower themselves slowly and steadily over a period by pain-stakingly extending their mucal strings. When some critical distance is reached, they entwine first of all their mucal strings and then themselves, both upside down, and then their shiny white reproductive parts. Mating then takes place as normal – normal, that is, for love-darting hermaphrodites – and can last up to an hour. After this, one slug just drops off down to the ground while the other climbs back up the mucal string, eating it as it goes. I suppose it feels quite peckish after all its exertions. Amazing. All this activity going on in the garden while we sleep easily in our beds.

What else is disporting itself out in the garden under the cover of darkness? Earthworms, if you look closely, seem to live strange and exotic lives too when viewed from our perspective. For a start, they have no eyes, so you'd wonder why day or night makes any difference to them. They live in the soil and eat the dead plant material that is mixed up with the soil particles. However, to get at these, they have to eat the soil and digest out the food particles as they pass through their bodies. So they don't need eyes, they live in the middle of their food and just eat their way around, tunnelling through their food supply. But it's a lonely life down there and worm does not live by bread alone, as it were. At night, when it is cool and dark, they come up to the surface, up into the garden, to suss out the social scene. Although they have no eyes, they do have light receptors in their skin, so they can determine if it is still dark. They hate the light, as it fills them with fears of being heated up and dried out, not to mention being breakfast for those pesky early birds who are on the rampage the minute the first photon of light appears. No, they risk all coming up to the surface to meet other earthworms, although not ones of the opposite sex. Earthworms, like molluscs, are hermaphrodites, and have both male and female organs. Unlike the snails, however, they mate, as it were, one upside-down, the other right way round. Allow me to explain such *Kama Sutra*-like behaviour.

A worm's body is a series of segments. Number one is up near the head and number one hundred and fifty is down at the other end. The male organs are at segments nine, ten and eleven and the female organs are at segments thirteen and fourteen. (Are you with me so far?) Further along the worm's body, at segments thirty-two to thirty-seven, we come to a remarkable organ called the clitellum. It looks for all the world like a saddle on the worm's body. This produces an exceedingly sticky mucus, which is vital to the whole mating process. A typical encounter might go like this. An amorous earthworm, who has risked all in the pursuit of love, tunnels its way to the surface one dark, damp night. It slithers blindly around in the grass until it encounters another earthworm with similar intentions. Presumably it is able to distinguish between slugs and worms – I'm sure they must feel quite different, and anyway the slug, which can see, would be able to give the worm a wide berth. So having encountered the love of its life, our earthworm has to ascertain whether it is coming or going. It then sticks its clitellum (at segments thirty-two to thirty-seven, remember) to segments nine to fifteen of the other worm, and arranges the rest of itself so that its reproductive organs are glued to the other's clitellum. This would all seem to require a remarkable amount of co-operation and dexterity.

Then they begin to mate. One worm produces sperm at segments ten and eleven. This trickles down its own body in a special groove, until it comes to where its clitellum is firmly glued to the body of the other worm. The sperm then makes the crossing at this point into the body of the other worm at segment nine. Meanwhile, the other worm is doing exactly the same thing in the other direction. It is not a speedy process. It can take up to five hours, and if the dawn comes before the job is complete they could be caught in the act by a starving thrush who would get two for the price of one, or at least one anyway as they struggle to detach and slither away. Such a violent end would break a worm's heart, a not insignificant procedure, seeing as how worms have not one, but five hearts.

However, we will not contemplate such a nasty end for our worms, but assume that they manage to complete the business, disentangle tenderly and glide slowly away to their underground world before the sun comes up. A few days later, the clitellum springs into action again. It covers itself with a hard coat, detaches itself entirely from segments thirty-two to thirty-seven and begins to move up along the worm's body, segment by segment. As it passes segment fourteen it collects its own eggs that are waiting there and continues on its journey. As it passes segment nine, it picks up the sperm the other worm left there during the mating process and fertilisation of the eggs takes place in the clitellum during the last bit of the journey up to segment one. Sort of test-tube fertilisation, as it were. The clitellum now comes off the worm completely and is shed into the soil where it looks like a tiny yellow lemon. Only one of the fertilised eggs develops into a baby worm. This grows for up to three weeks in its clitellum swaddling clothes, and then it is ready to face the world as a fully fledged worm. Wouldn't you know that worms, which are good for our soil and more than earn their keep breaking down dead plants, only reproduce one at a time, whereas slugs and snails, which wreak havoc on our delicate garden treasures, can lay up to one hundred eggs at a time, *all* of which hatch out into new slugs or snails. It's just not fair.

Is it all just one big orgy that is going on in the garden at night under the cover of darkness? Well, there is a fair bit of violence and murder going on as well. The carnivores are using the cover of darkness to leap upon an unsuspecting meal. Centipedes can be particularly voracious hunters. These are misnamed creatures, as they rarely have a hundred legs exactly. Many of the fast-hunting garden ones have only fifteen pairs of legs, while some of the blind, burrowing ones can have up to eighty-three pairs of legs. But they all have poison claws just behind the head, which enable them to kill their prey very quickly. The garden centipede has about twenty-five tiny eyes on each side of its head, so it can get about very nicely at night. As one might expect, it catches and eats insects that are unwary enough to be in its way, but it can also catch and eat worms and slugs and is not above a spot of cannibalism if another centipede crosses its path. They are not waterproof and

WILD AND WONDERFUL

often lurk under flowerpots during the day to avoid drying out, but you'll notice, if you lift one suddenly and stay alert, that there is always only one centipede per flowerpot. Be careful if you are handling the bigger ones, because they are not above attacking us with their poison claws and these are sometimes strong enough to pierce the skin and inflict quite a nip. But if you hate slugs in the garden you will overlook such bad-tempered tendencies and rank the centipedes among the good guys.

In fact, if any enemy of the slug is a friend of yours, then you should grapple all the members of the ground beetle family to your soul with hoops of steel. Don't be calling this lot cockroaches, no matter how much television you watch. Cockroaches – the real ones – are not native to Ireland and cannot exist in the garden in the wild. They live in countries much warmer than ours, such as America and the countries of southern Europe, and are occasionally brought here by an unwary traveller. They can become established indoors, where it is always warm – places with the central heating always on, such as in hospitals, laundries, warehouses, factories, hotels, even in homes if you are very *flaithiúlach* with the heating, but hunting out in your garden at night – not so. You will always know a cockroach no matter what colour it is because it has enormous antennae. These emerge from their heads and curve around like whips and extend back halfway along the length of their bodies. And they are not hunters. They eat leftover food and insects that are already dead. No, the dramatic, exciting creature is not the cockroach but the ground beetle, who is on the rampage in your garden under the cover of darkness on a seek-and-exterminate mission.

The deadliest, the most cunning, the most ruthless, the most devious of them all is the devil's coach-horse, the largest of the rove beetle family. It is jet black and can be up to an inch long. Like all rove beetles, it has ferocious jaws, with which it eats slugs, caterpillars and any other small creature that has the misfortune to cross its path. It has a long, thinnish body, because, unlike other beetle groups, the front wings are not modified into roundy wing covers that cover the rest of its body. It has quite small upper wing cases, but it has functional back wings and can fly about terrorising the other garden inhabitants. When it meets something much bigger than itself, it is not above a spot of intimidation. It opens wide its jaws, cocks up its tail and squirts a little strong-smelling vapour in the face of the enemy. Certainly a creature you'd prefer to have as a friend rather than as a foe.

There are other interesting beetles wandering around the garden at night. People often ask where do all the dead birds' bodies go, as they are rarely seen just lying about. Injured birds often crawl away under bushes to die in the first place and then their freshly dead corpses are just lying there as a succulent treat for the burying beetles and the sexton beetles the following night. These beetles generally wander around looking for a dead body. They have a good sense of smell and soon locate just such a treat. The first one of each sex that arrives on the scene fights off all comers of the same sex. When the first one of the opposite sex arrives, the mood changes. The presence of all this smelly food inspires them with uncontrollable lust and they quickly mate. Having got that over with, they proceed to the main business – that of burying the body. They do this by removing the soil from underneath it so that it slowly sinks beneath the ground. They are well able to cut any impeding grass roots with their jaws and soon all that can be seen of the dead bird is a slight mound above the ground surface. The female then excavates a small tunnel leading off from the burial chamber and lays her eggs there. She is a very devoted mother and stands by while the eggs hatch out, feeding herself from the buried body. She brings chewed-up bird to the young while they are quite tiny and cannot fend for themselves, but soon they can smell where the food is coming from and they head off to dine themselves. With such an abundant supply of food, they quickly grow and get on to the next stage of their life cycle. They undergo three changes, ending up as a legless maggot. They then abandon the by-now nearly demolished carcass, burrow deeper and pupate into adults. They subsequently emerge and wander around the garden looking for a meal, a fight, a girlfriend and a good time, quite typical adolescent behaviour really.

There is one exciting beetle that we don't have in our gardens, at least not yet, and that is the glow-worm. These are beetles that do occur in Britain in areas of chalk and limestone and they rejoice in the Latin name of *Lampyris*. While we have such terrain in Ireland too, these creatures obviously never made it here under their own steam after the Ice Age. As only the males can fly, I suppose they would have had to give the females a piggyback if they were to establish breeding colonies in our island country. These beetles give out light from their bodies, but it is the adult female which gives out the most light of all. In the underside of her last three abdominal segments she has a large supply of luciferin, backed by a reflector of minute crystals. When oxygen and water are supplied to this area by the female, the three segments glow brightly with a pale greenish-blue light. This is such a concentration of effort that females have no wings or wing cases at all, and look for all the world like woodlice. When night comes and they are ready for action, they climb up on a blade of grass or a plant, send down the oxygen and water and raise their abdomen. The males who have wings and large, light-sensitive eyes are of course cruising the area looking out for just such a signal. She doesn't have to wave her light for long before he arrives. If, however, the light attracts the wrong kind of client, she can immediately extinguish it, so you couldn't quickly gather a jam jar full to light the way if the flashlight on your bike failed. Still, the lights will come back on again if one or two are left gently in a box for a while.

Like adult butterflies, adult glow-worms hardly feed at all, but their larval offspring make up for this. They feed on both snails and slugs in a particularly ghoulish fashion.

They grab the poor little snails and slugs in their strong jaws and inject a digestive juice. This first of all paralyses the prey and then – horror of horrors! – begins to dissolve its flesh, which can then be drunk by the larvae. Maybe it's just as well we haven't got such creatures in this country. Do we hate our molluscs that much?

Fireflies are beetles of the same family, which occur in the tropics. The female adults with the luminous underparts can fly there, hence the name fireflies.

So in our gardens we may well have sex and drugs and rock'n'roll but, in true Irish fashion, no light is shed upon the matter. It is all conducted under the cover of darkness.

THE ONES THAT GOT AWAY

WHEN MY BOOK *Talking Wild* came out, I got letters from readers who were disappointed that I had not covered the particular creepy-crawlies that they were interested in, revolted by, intrigued with. I, of course, had cherry-picked and had only included the ones that I felt everyone would know and identify with – in a manner of speaking. And as we have at least 16,000 creepy-crawlies – or, to give them a more scientific title, invertebrates – in Ireland, that's all I am about to do this time too.

Silverfish are weird-looking things. People encounter them late at night when they go back downstairs for a drink of water and surprise them slithering around the kitchen sink. Someone asked me recently if silverfish were the nearest thing to a dinosaur that we had, which rather took me aback for a moment. After all, dinosaurs were reptiles, sometimes absolutely huge and indeed are now extinct, whereas silverfish are tiny little insects that are very much with us. But the connection would seem to be that silverfish are very ancient and primitive insects that have remained unchanged for millions of year and would indeed have been around at the time of the dinosaurs. They are silvery in colour and appear to us to move by slithering around wettish areas and so seem more like fish than the insects they are. They have no wings but have six tiny legs and three tails and two antennae straight out of their heads like horns, if you are in a mood to admire them. They belong to a group of insects called bristletails.

They are not a favourite of our listeners, however, and indeed samples in matchboxes come with the invariable plea: what is this and how do you get rid of it? Well, it's a silverfish and to get rid of it − or indeed of anything unwanted − you have to understand why it is there in the first place. If you are giving it food and excellent living quarters − no matter how inadvertently − of course you will have it in abundance. So what does it need to live? Well, first of all it needs your house − these are purely domestic insects and cannot survive out in the open. They like warm, damp conditions, so they frequent kitchens and bathrooms. They only appear at night − they apparently sleep during the day and come out for food after dark. They seem to love glue and wallpaper paste, so if there are any cracks around the sink – loose wallpaper that the damp has caused to come away from the wall, loose or cracked tiles that they can get in behind, an area where the sink is not exactly flush with the wall – well, they are at their granny's: food and damp and hiding places all at once. They will also live in food cupboards, feasting on bits of paper, carton glue and, as a great bonus, spilt flour. Actually, if you are going to leave spilt flour in your food cupboard for any length of time, you could do a PhD thesis on the creepy-crawlies that come to dine.

If you don't like them, ask yourself why. They are not dirty and don't carry disease. There is no smell from them. They didn't wreck the place and vandalise the tiles in the first place – they just came to live in the already broken tile. Stay out of the kitchen at night and you won't see them. Otherwise, you will have to do up your sink area – new tiles, waterproof paper, new grouting and sealant – and that will starve them out. Or get the landlord to do up the place: they are often encountered in bedsits.

They have a relation called the firebrat, which is able to withstand much higher temperatures and can be found around hot-water pipes. This is, however, quite rare and is hardly ever complained of. Perhaps our nocturnal wanderings to the hot press are much less frequent than our midnight forays to the kitchen.

Bed bugs also featured in *Talking Wild*. They were just one of a myriad of creatures that could beset our person and indeed one of the less nasty types, I said. Even though they do bite us in bed, they do not carry disease. Fleas and body lice were much worse. But then a listener phoned in about strange creatures she had in her house – kind of like ladybirds without spots. Some type of woodworm she had acquired in a bed she had bought, she supposed it was. Would we come and look? Well, we came and looked – at a massive invasion of bedbugs that had even spread next door, and the resultant postbag, after we broadcast the item, would have put Liveline to shame. People from all over were writing in confessing that they too had bedbugs and they had never been able to talk about them before. Such shame was associated with them, that they felt decent, god-fearing folk would shun them. One especially long missive had the address cut off the top of the letter; obviously the writer had had second thoughts before posting it.

What was abundantly clear from all the letters was how persistent they were and how difficult it was to get rid of them. As they only come out at night to bite, there is no sign of them during the day. But they lay tiny eggs in rough timber, such as down cracks in floorboards and on the unplaned wood behind bedboards. Pest removal companies come and spray and fumigate, but short of throwing everything in the room out (through the bedroom window so that nothing drops off on the way through the house), they seem to be really impossible to exterminate. And indeed the psychological damage seems to be the worst. How can you know they are gone? The test is to make yourself into a sacrificial victim, sleep in the room and see if you get bitten – just the conditions to enable you to drop off into a deep sleep at once and stay asleep all night. They may have been brought to your house in furniture or they may have come with visitors, but one thing is certain – once news of their residence in your house gets out, visitors will vanish like snow off a ditch.

Certainly while Derek and myself were doing the 'Answering Machine Mission' in the house where they were first reported, we experienced mild disquiet. We were intrepid reporters on the job and I took back samples in a jar to confirm identification. However, I made sure that the jar rested for several days in my freezer before taking the beasties out to examine them with my hand lens and, confirming they were bedbugs, I disposed of the bodies afterwards with the care one would lavish on victims of the bubonic plague.

People are very good observers of wildlife when the wildlife is an unwanted occupant of their home. For some obscure reason, I am associated in the public mind with spiders, so people long to regale me with tales of their particular spider-infested home. Judging from the descriptions, a particularly obvious spider has taken up residence in homes in recent years. This spider has a small enough nondescript body, but by gum it has mighty legs. In fact it is often described as a daddy-long-legs spider and indeed that is one of the nicknames of *Pholcus phalangioides,* also known as the cellar spider. Now this spider has a great ability to spin webs in the corner of rooms, whether you are living there or not. They could be employed if one was creating a set for Miss Havisham's room in Dickens's *Great Expectations*. They are quite easy to see if you go to inspect any such web. The unusual thing about them is the frenzy they go into if you disturb them, however. They behave like whirling dervishes, bouncing up and down so fast that they become a blur.

We filmed one a few years ago for a series called *Habitats*. This programme visited various wildlife habitats and featured all the interesting filmable wildlife there. In the house-as-a-wildlife habitat we encountered such a spider, which was fairly uncommon at the time. I remember we affixed the poor creature to the wall with bits of Blu-Tack so that it could be filmed. I noticed, on my most recent visit to the house last year, the bits of Blu-Tack were still there, but not the spider itself. No doubt it had long since shuffled off this mortal coil, as small Irish spiders would be lucky to live for twelve months. They are much more frequently encountered now. A free fly-killing service – what more could you want?

CARNIVAL OF THE CARNIVORES

FOXES HAVE AN UNEASY relationship with humans at the best of times. What infuriates the owners of hens is the havoc the fox wreaks if it gets into the henhouse. It sidles in and, when the hens become aware of it, there is consternation. They all squawk and fly about in a panic. And this excites the fox into attacking and attacking until every last one is killed. He cannot possibly eat them all, but he kills and destroys wantonly, and no one else can eat them either. No wonder hen owners hate foxes. But what is really happening here is that the fox's natural hunting instincts are coming to the fore. In the days long before henhouses, a fox would be likely to come upon a sleeping roost of birds at night. Immediately upon attack, the birds would wake up and fly away. The fox's natural instinct would be to attack and kill as quickly as possible before they were all gone. He'd be lucky to get one or two. But in the henhouse, because there is a roof, the hens can't fly away and the panic, noise and clamour have the fox in a killing frenzy. Maybe the solution is a roofless henhouse, or exceedingly calm, placid hens.

Foxes get killed on the roads too, but not as many as badgers. Or maybe it's just that we don't see them because they are light enough to be thrown into the hedge by the speeding vehicle, as opposed to the heavier badger, which lands with a thump on the road itself. Or perhaps it is that the foxes are smart enough to run away when they hear vehicles approaching so that they don't get dazzled by the headlights.

In the 1950s and 1960s, a bounty could be claimed for every fox that was killed. The tail had to be handed in, no doubt to prevent a bounty being claimed over and over again for the same animal. It didn't make a blind bit of difference. Fox populations never went into a decline, and they are still quite plentiful. Their numbers are controlled by the amount of food that is available and the few that get killed for a bounty (or indeed that are taken by fox hunts) means that there is more food for those left behind and so more of their offspring will survive. It takes a really big reduction in their food supply, like myxomatosis in rabbits, before fox numbers noticeably drop. On the other hand, foxes will never wipe out a thriving colony of bunnies, because rabbits can breed faster than foxes can kill them.

Foxes are scavengers too, which means that they will eat meat that they have not killed themselves. Much of the mutton found in the stomachs of foxes was mutton before the fox ever came across it. Newborn lambs often die of the cold, particularly if they are born early in a cold spring, and foxes will certainly eat their dead remains. There was great excitement in the spring of 2004 with the invention of plastic coats for lambs, which kept them from getting cold and wet and also rustled and smelt strange to marauding foxes. They certainly reduced the mortality in newborn lambs, for whatever reason.

City people generally like foxes, as they get glimpses of them in their gardens at dawn or at dusk. We are rarely if ever asked how to get rid of them from city areas, though in fact there are more urban foxes now than there are in rural areas, as it is easier for a fox to make a living in our suburban sprawl. They are supremely intelligent creatures and can adapt to new sources of food easily. They know that our bins contain food-laden rubbish. They can manage to flip the lids of over-filled wheelie bins and extract whatever chicken bones and half eaten pizzas have been deposited inside. But what I hadn't realised was that foxes in Dublin could not only read, but could read Irish. At least the ones in Terenure can. When I was doing my civic duty on the residents' association committee, my neighbours felt that they could bring their environmental problems to my doorstep for resolution. So, one evening, one of my neighbours came around to report that the area was going to the dogs. Why, even his morning delivery of milk was not safe from light-fingered gurriers who had nothing better to do than to go round stealing the milk of law-abiding citizens. It struck me as strange that gurriers would be up at 6.30 in the morning stealing milk, so I asked him, reasonably I felt, how he knew it was gurriers. Had he actually seen them at it? Well, no. So I suggested that the thing to do was get the milkman to ring the doorbell as he delivered the milk and the neighbour should come down and conduct a stakeout on the milk, to see exactly what was happening. I thought that would be the end of it, and that I would hear no more about it.

Of course not. He was round again the next night with the next instalment of the tale. The milkman left the milk and rang the doorbell. Your man leapt out of bed and hastened downstairs. He was just in time to see a fox come round the side of the house, seize the milk in its jaws and return back to whence it came – the overgrown, neglected garden next door. There the fox ripped open the carton, drank the milk and proceeded to suckle her cubs who were waiting for her. And strewn around were the remains of many other cartons, which had featured on my neighbour's milk bill, if not his breakfast table. How did the fox know there was milk in the carton in the first instance? Sure, wasn't *bainne* written on it – that's how.

So I asked my neighbour what was he going to do. He

said that he would get the milkman to put the milk inside his glass porch and close the door, and he was going to come downstairs the next morning to see the look on the fox's face when it beheld the unavailable milk. Poor Reynard!

Another favourite among city dwellers is the hedgehog. Whether the story of Mrs Tiggywinkle is indelibly imprinted in our minds or what, certainly callers to the programme are much more anxious to acquire a hedgehog than to seek to get rid of one. Hedgehogs are not native to Ireland. This means that they were not among the select few that made it to these parts under their own steam after the last ice age. They were, it seems, brought here by the Danes as a source of food. Apparently they were killed, covered in clay and baked in the embers of a fire. You then peeled off the baked clay, skin, spines and all, and the meat tasted like pork. Anyway, do not be tempted to try such a dish – hedgehogs are now protected here under the Wildlife Act. They are great travellers, and if you find one in your garden it does not necessarily mean that it has taken up residence there. It is much more likely just to be passing through. Why people want them so much seems amazing, given that they are covered in fleas, which may well hop off the creature and give you a bite, before copping on that you are the wrong host – oops, sorry!

Hedgehogs feed on slugs and snails, and if there is one group of creatures at the top of every gardener's hate list, it is the aforementioned molluscs. A hedgehog in the garden is considered a great asset, as they will definitely keep snail and slug numbers down. Certain people have been known to stop their cars at night if they encounter hedgehogs on the road, get out and wrap the creature up in the car mat and take it home to the garden. And if it is a walled, enclosed garden, it may well stay, as it can't climb directly up walls to escape.

If the temperature drops suddenly in October, hedgehogs go into hibernation for the winter. They find a heap of old leaves under the garden shed or wherever and roll up into a ball, lower their metabolic rate and sleep until springtime. So you have to be very careful raking leaves in November not to inadvertently disturb them in their slumbers. It takes such a lot of energy to raise their body temperature back to normal levels and to increase their breathing and heart rate, that they won't have enough stores of fat to last till spring if you do.

Our listeners have brought a phenomenon to our attention about hedgehogs that may well be linked to climate change. Normal hedgehogs in normal circumstances have their young in June. They have all summer long to feed them and teach them how to feed for themselves. This is important, as hedgehogs less than a pound (about 450 grams) in weight do not have enough energy laid down in the form of fat to last the winter. But recently our listeners are reporting babies born in September – a second family perhaps, the female being stimulated to breed again because of our warmer summer nights. But these babies have very little time to put on condition, and when the cold of Hallowe'en comes, will not have enough fuel in the tank, as it were, to survive hibernation. Kind garden owners would like to feed such hedgehogs and this is a good idea. Do not, however feed them with bread and milk, no matter what Enid Blyton says. They are not calves but carnivores and they need meat. Tins of meaty dogfood are the business. Put this out for them every evening, with just plain water if you like, and this will surely help. You could, of course, collect a nice bucket of slugs for dessert if you were in the humour.

So fond are people of hedgehogs that they do not want to hear any bad-news stories about them. So the story about the harm the hedgehogs were doing on the Hebrides in Scotland went down like a lead balloon with some of our listeners. Hedgehogs had been brought on to some of these islands deliberately by people who wanted them in their gardens. But being wanderers, they didn't necessarily stay in the gardens eating slugs, but went on a wander over the whole place. And those islands are particularly important as refuges for nesting seabirds in summer – seabirds that build their nests on the ground. Wandering hedgehogs found these nests and saw the eggs as a very delicious source of food. Their numbers increased and multiplied, but not those of the seabirds, which were alas being decimated by the hedgehogs. Natural enemies of the hedgehogs are badgers, foxes, ten-ton trucks and pesticides used in gardens. None of these were particularly common on these Scottish islands, so the checks and balances that normally occur weren't there. So it was decided to cull the inadvisedly introduced hedgehogs, in the interest of the seabirds, which were rapidly becoming endangered. But people with gardens in hedgehogless parts of Britain thought, 'such a waste, why can't we have them in our gardens? We'd love them'. So there were the pros and the antis for hedgehog resettlement.

Why were there no hedgehogs in these gardens in the first place, if they were being touted as such good homes? The surroundings patently aren't suitable. On the other hand, taking your chances in a garden in the home counties surely is better than definite death at the hands of the cullers.

But why not introduce something into the islands that will naturally predate the hedgehogs, you might ask, and that would solve the problem. *What*? And make a bad story worse, when these hedgehog-eaters turn their attention to the seabirds as well? There are no easy answers. In fact I wonder are there any answers at all.

It was proving quite difficult to catch the hedgehogs on the islands, dead or alive, when we carried the story on the programme. It just goes to show that, usually, introducing a species of anything where it has not come by itself and established a balance naturally is A Bad Thing. We have so many examples of this here in Ireland – rhododendron in the Killarney woodlands, giant hogweed along our water-ways, magpies, I suppose, in our suburbia, zebra mussels in our waterways, New Zealand flatworms in our soil, mink in our rivers, not to speak of rats and house mice which nobody wants. The list is endless. We just can't learn to leave well enough alone.

The only land carnivore whose private life hasn't been revealed yet is the pygmy shrew, so why should I leave you with an incomplete picture? This is our smallest mammal by a long shot – it is only between forty and sixty millimetres long and weighs only three grams in spring after a hard winter. When you consider that this is about the size and weight of the body of a large hawk moth and that mice are veritable monsters by comparison, having a head and body length of one hundred millimetres and weighing in at twenty-five grams, you can appreciate how tiny they are. They are extremely common and widespread according to distribution records, but most people have never seen one, unless they have a cat. Cats – the horrible things – kill little creatures for fun, and then, as they don't in the least want to eat them, will often bring them in to their doting owners as presents. Pygmy shrews often feature on the present list.

Shrews live in fields, hedges, bogs and woodlands and are to be seen all the year round as they don't hibernate. Strangely for something so small, it is believed that this is one of our native mammals and that it managed to get here before the land bridges broke. There are no bones in the archaeological remains, but then they are so tiny and brittle, shrew bones wouldn't have survived. DNA analysis would give their breed, seed and generation for definite, so there's a project for an aspiring zoologist.

Pygmy shrews are welcome visitors to the gardens of those who are less than passionate about beetles, woodlice and spiders, and in turn are on the menus of owls and foxes who are not put off by the horrible smell that comes from their scent glands. You would imagine that, being so tiny, they would be very delicate and graceful feeders, just nibbling at their food. So you might think it to be a compliment to tell someone they eat like a pygmy shrew. Not so. Pygmy shrews eat their own weight in food every day and will die of starvation if deprived of food for more than three hours. So they are, in fact, real gobble guts. They have to feed by day and by night to keep going. They make a very definite squeaking noise and indeed are more often heard than seen.

They are the only shrew species we have here. Indeed, we have very few small mammals compared to Britain or mainland Europe – having only the pygmy shrew itself, two species of mice and the bank vole, which apparently was introduced to County Limerick in the 1960s. No wonder we only have two resident owl species – there's not a great variety of food for them to pick and choose from at night.

Top carnivores, at the top of their food chain, are – would you believe it? – ladybirds. Very few things eat ladybirds because they are full of formic acid and taste horrible. They exude this horrible tasting, smelly liquid through their legs and any inexperienced bird that may have it in its mouth at this time quickly drops it. The frog is perhaps the only thing in this country that can bring itself to swallow a ladybird, and even then only when the poor frog is desperate. But at least ladybirds have the decency to warn any would-be predator of their horribleness, by being brightly coloured. They do not skulk away and hide in vegetation, but broadcast their presence to the world.

As well as red ones with black spots, we have black ones with red spots, yellow ones, orange ones and brown ones. In fact, we have eighteen species in all in Ireland. There is a Dublin ladybird which is red with two black spots, one on each side. Because the city, with all its concrete, has a warmer microclimate than the rest of the country, this creature is able to survive here quite happily in urban gardens. It is smaller than its culchie relation, the seven-spot, another red ladybird with black spots, which is common in rural gardens. In fact, this one occurs in city gardens too, which must be the reason for the confusion people have about them. I am often told that ladybirds acquire more spots as they get older. Presumably, Dublin residents see the two species in their gardens and think that one is an older version of the other. This is not so: they are separate and distinct species.

We like ladybirds because they are red, which seems to us, if not to the birds, to be a friendly colour. They also please us by dining extensively on aphids, particularly greenflies, which are such a pest on roses. It has been estimated by people who find such matters riveting that a single ladybird will eat five and a half thousand greenflies over a season in your garden. Even more riveting, they have estimated that there will be nine separate generations of greenflies in your garden over a summer. So one greenfly in your garden at the start of the summer – and only one female is needed: this lot don't need men at all, the ultimate feminists – will give rise to 600 million aphids in your garden if left unchecked. So three cheers then for hordes of hungry ladybirds.

Ladybirds are actually beetles, in the same group as the devil's coach-horse and the big black clocks that people hate so much because, they say, they 'look horrible'. It's amazing what a touch of lipstick and rouge will do in the popularity stakes, but then, we women always knew that anyway!

SHE FINDS SEASHELLS ON THE **SEASHORE**

THE SEASHORE IS A whole magical world where there is a possibility that anything could turn up. The tides pound on it and then retreat, so everything washed up by the sea is there for the inspection of the first curious creature that comes along. After storms and high tides is the best time for beachcombing, as the turbulent sea may have cast up God-knows-what kind of treasures from its depths. But really, anyone with any bit of curiosity and half an eye can always find something of interest on the seashore, even on the calmest day.

There are always shells. These are, or in most cases were, the homes of sea animals from the mollusc group – in other words, the sea-dwelling cousins of our more familiar snails. Usually the shells are empty, because the inhabitants, who would have lived somewhere else in the sea-dominated world, have died and their empty home has been washed up by the surf. There is a whole area of study devoted to shells – conchology – and there are many, many shells to warrant this amount of interest.

When I was a child (me and Fionn Mac Cumhaill it seems now, describing it to the present generation of young people) we used to spend our summers in Clogherhead in County Louth. Long days were spent on the beach – in true golden-hued memory, the sun always shone – and the main occupation was building sandcastles. These were always decorated with shells, and we had a great system of sorting them out according to their perceived enhancement of the completed castle. First up for usefulness was the pelican's foot shell. This is a lovely square shell with two points on the two top corners. It graced the walls surrounding the castle wonderfully and there were always loads of them. Imagine my chagrin when, years later, now in the position of supervisor to the castle-building activities of my own children on west-coast beaches, not a single pelican's foot shell could be located for wall enhancement. It turns out that the sandy coast of Louth and Meath is the main area where these shells turn up and, while there are plenty of adornments for sandcastles on the west-coast beaches, the pelican's foot is not one of them.

This shell is the home of a snail-like creature, and like

many another whose shell is familiar to us, such as cockles and razor shells, it lives burrowed down in the mud at the bottom of the sea near to the shore. It feeds by sticking up a part of its body into the surrounding water and drawing in food from that. When the animal dies, the shell works loose and is washed in by the tide. While pelican's feet come in single shells only, as it were, cockles and razor shells are bivalves and the animal is protected by two shells that close. After death and the subsequent pounding by the sea, the two halves quite often part and we only find a single cockle or a single razor shell. Mussels, scallops, oysters and clams are all bivalves, and the shells of all of these turn up frequently on the shore, empty alas, as these are all good to eat.

The pelican's foot is a univalve mollusc with one shell only, the same general blueprint as our land snail. Other univalve shells that end up on the high-tide mark may have spent their lives on quite a different shore. The limpet, which looks like a conical hat, is a sort of mini-cow in its eating habits. It grazes the green algae that grow on the surfaces of rocks on the shore. It moves about feeding when the tide is in and sticks on really fast when the tide is out. Empty limpet shells can adorn a sandy beach, depending on tides and currents. Periwinkles are univalves that can appear in quite a range of colours. There is also a mother-of-pearl type of univalve with lovely tortoiseshell colours on the outside and shiny mother-of-pearl-coloured lining, which turns up on sandy shores from time to time. It is shaped for all the world like an old-fashioned spinning top that people who were young along with Fionn Mac Cumhaill – oh, forty years ago at least – used to play with. These shells are not unsurprisingly known as top shells and their live, snail-like bodies contain a glorious purple dye, fit for the robes of emperors and cardinals. They were collected for this very purpose historically, but they were never eaten, as the colour makes the flesh of the snail therein poisonous.

Like any division of the animal kingdom, there are carnivores in this group as well. Whelks look like a heavily embossed univalve grazer, but this heavy armour in their shell is not there for nothing. These are carnivores and they feed by drilling a hole through the shell of their unsuspecting targets and sucking out the flesh within. Dog whelks drill holes in barnacles, which cannot escape, as they are cemented fast to the rocks. These also contain purple dye and were harvested on the Iniskea islands for their colour in Neolithic times. The sting winkle, also known as the oyster drill, hangs around oyster beds, drilling holes in oysters. The common whelk shell turns up frequently on our beaches as well. It seems to end up in the bottom of small rock pools, and if you put your hand in to take one out, you might be startled to see legs coming out of it and it running off. A left-behind cartoon creature from some Disney rock-pool movie? No, it is just a hermit crab which has taken up residence in an empty shell and is moving off out of danger. Hermit crabs have shell-covered front claws like any other crab, but there the resemblance ends. The rest of its body is soft-skinned, with no shell protecting it. It makes good the deficiency by squatting in a whelk shell. This is all fine as long as the shell fits. But the hermit crab continues to grow, the space becomes tighter in the shell, and the time comes for a bigger suit. Can you imagine the worry and stress? Another, bigger, empty whelk shell has to be found, so that the transfer can be effected. Do you go looking for one, or hope one will turn up on the next tide? Will it be empty? Do hermit crabs haul each other out of shells and stage a takeover bid? Not so, apparently. They eventually happen on a bigger empty shell, and you would think all their worries are over. Not at all. The worst is yet to come. The hermit crab has to withdraw from its current cramped quarters and reverse into the bigger home. This must be done in a thrice, as there is any amount of creatures that would dearly love the unprotected rear end of a hermit crab between shells. There must be a monumental sigh of relief when it is safely ensconced in its new quarters. Surely this kind of carry-on must be the greatest possible deterrent to putting on weight.

But it is not only shells you will find on the seashore. Jellyfish get washed up as well. The one most commonly seen is – surprise, surprise – the common jellyfish. This is a transparent jellyfish the size of a fried egg, although they can sometimes grow up to a foot in diameter. In the centre of the clear jelly circle as you look down at it, there are four dark purple horse-shoe-shaped rings. These are its reproductive parts. Turn it over, however (with a stick, or the

toe of your boot, *not* with your hand), and you will see the
stinging tentacles attached to its underside. These hang
down as the jellyfish undulates through the water in life like
a swimming umbrella. They sting and paralyse any small
prey it comes across, which are then scooped up as food.
Don't be fooled. Just because the thing is lying here on the
beach apparently dead doesn't mean that the tentacles
have lost their sting. They have not – hence the advice not to
handle it. In fact, you can get quite a nasty sting across the
face while swimming from the tentacle of a jellyfish which
has been cut off from the jelly body by a boat's propeller
and thus is invisible in the water. While this is the most
common jellyfish you are likely to see on the beach, you
could come across others. A yellowy brown one with a
coloured edge is the compass jellyfish. Tiny purple ones
about three inches long are often washed up in hundreds
on beaches on the south and west coasts in the summer,
prompting queries from curious and observant listeners.
These are called by-the-wind sailors (the jellyfish, not the
listeners), because they consist of a flat disc with a vertical
'sail' on top and short tentacles underneath. These live in
warmer waters than ours, but are carried north in ocean
currents and get washed up on our beaches. The one to
avoid like the plague is its much larger brother – the
Portuguese man-o'-war. The Portuguese must have been a
fearsome lot to meet on the high seas in their sailing ships
equipped for battle, seeing as how they have given their
name to this jellyfish-like creature. Like the by-the-wind

sailor, it has a disc-like oval body and a 'sail' sticking up out of the top to catch the wind and float on ocean currents. It is huge in comparison to the sailor – its body can be a foot long – but the dangerous bits are the tentacles, which stream out behind it and can be up to three feet in length. They carry extremely dangerous stings, so there is usually great drama if one is washed up or is seen in the water. Again, they are inhabitants of warmer waters, but they do end up here occasionally and may indeed increase in frequency if our waters warm significantly for them.

Another seashore creature that can cause hysterics and lots of column inches in the silly season is the not-a-bit-silly weever fish. These are small shallow-water fish that bury themselves in the mud and muddy sand just at the water's edge. They have sharp fins that stick up out of their backs – dorsal fins – and fins covering their gills on either side of their heads. They sneakily lie buried in the muddy sand, which of course is the exact colour of themselves, with these nasty spiny fins upright. Anyone paddling at the water's edge who has the misfortune to step on one in their bare feet will feel the most painful sting ever. This painful sting is practically unbearable and the victim gets a terrible fright. The way to deal with it is to let it bleed as much as it will and then to bathe the foot in the very hottest water possible. Nobody dies from this, but the pain is awful, so that if there is a case of this by the seaside in summer it always makes the local papers. Not a nice thing to encounter at the water's edge.

Amid the other flotsam and jetsam washed up on the high-tide mark, you may encounter mermaid's purses, cuttlebones, whelk egg cases that look like polystyrene and, depending on the sophistication of the dirty-water treatment plant in the area, some of the plastic items that people stupidly buy and then even more stupidly flush down the loo. Actually, none of the objects listed there can strictly speaking be classified in this way. Flotsam is defined as wreckage found floating, whereas jetsam is actual cargo flung overboard from a ship, which has been jettisoned to lighten the load. Maybe we should invent a new word for stuff that gets into the sea without being part of a ship or her cargo. How about pollutsam?

Mermaid's purses are the egg cases of dogfish. They are brown rectangular capsules with a curly tendril coming out of each corner. Inside each one was a baby dogfish, and the tendrils were entwined around seaweed underneath the water as the baby inside grew and developed. But some were torn off by the cruel sea and washed ashore. Sometimes you can even see the little fish inside if you hold it up to the light. It is too late to put it back at this stage. The lad inside is *aimsir caite* by now.

The cuttlebone is like something you'd have in a bird's cage for it to sharpen its beak on, and indeed this is what it is used for. It started out life as the skeleton of a cuttlefish, which is a lesser-known member of the group that includes octopus and squid. While the squid has a scaffold in its bag to keep it rigid, which looks and feels for all the world like a piece of clear plastic, the cuttlefish has this oval, shell-like structure made of calcium. It is all that survives the death of the cuttlefish and so ends up on the shore.

Whelk egg cases are like yellow bubblewrap. It's hard to believe that they were once part of a living thing, but they were the maternity unit for the whelk, which may have donated its shell after death to the hermit crab in yonder rock pool. Go back and check, and while you are groping around trying to locate the shell that was there a few minutes ago, look at the edges of the rocks that are permanently submerged under the water. This is where the sea anemones live. These are red or occasionally green flowerlike lumps of jelly, stuck on to the sides of the pool. They are animals, not plants, and the nice-looking tentacles, which remind one of flower petals, are waving around in the water trying to guide tiny particles into the central mouth. Put your finger in the centre – go on, do. You will feel a slight suction as the poor anemone tries to draw in your finger. It hasn't a hope, but it's good fun to try.

If the rock pools are in limestone rocks, be careful where you put your knees. You don't want to kneel on a sea urchin! The ones encountered bored into rocks on shores in the west of Ireland are quite different from the grapefruit-sized white spheres that can be converted to lampshades by art-and-crafty types. The latter live on the seabed and are occasionally washed ashore, usually in bits. The ones that you want to avoid with your knees are much smaller and, as they are living on the seashore, are covered with a very spiny purple coat. The name sea urchin in English differ-entiates it from the land urchin – now, of course, known as the hedgehog. The sea urchins belong to a distinct family called echinoderms, of which starfish are also members. The spines are part of the living body and drop off when the creature dies. The French are very fond of them and they feature on seafood buffets there as *oursin*. If you are sure the water in which they live is clean, you can sample them for yourself. You need a strong knife to prise one out of its burrow. Turn it over and you are looking at its mouth. Open this with a flick of the knife (unless of course you are French, in which case you will possess a *coupe-oursin*), as if you were opening an egg. You can eat the surprisingly small amount of contents raw, just like that. They are orange in colour, star-shaped in design and what they are is the creature's reproductive parts. *Magnifique!* Why should the French hog this delicacy all to themselves?

CHAPTER NINETEEN

TIMBERRRRRR!

IRELAND IS ONE of the best countries in the world for the growing of trees; not that you would think so from the miserly total of native trees we have – twenty-eight in all. Why, a mere national park in Costa Rica has over three hundred native trees in an area the size of County Louth! Our mild, wet climate, with few full days below freezing in winter and few really dry scorching hot days in summer, makes for ideal tree-growing conditions. The arboretum in Wexford – the John F Kennedy Memorial Park – is testimony to this. Trees from every continent grow here happily, monkey puzzles from Chile cheek by jowl, as it were, with eucalyptus from Australia and ginkgo from China.

So why have we so few native trees? Well, it all goes back to the ice ages, which have been sweeping down over Europe for the last two million years. Because of the direction of our European mountain ranges, delicate species could not escape south ahead of the ice, nor could they return very quickly from further south during the inter-glacial spells. At the end of the last Ice Age, Ireland was only connected to Europe for a thousand years or so before the melting ice raised the sea levels to cut it off entirely. Whatever speedy tree species got here before then, that was it. And twenty-eight it was. Trees are not able to move themselves. (Although, that said, I did see a walking tree in the tropical forests of Costa Rica. And no I hadn't been at the blue Smarties! This tree grew by having a huge collection of thin trunks, rather as if it were being held up on a hundred stilts. And as time went by, the stilts on one side were more favoured than on the other side, so more of them grew there, while the unfavoured ones on the other side died off. So over its lifetime, the tree might move in the favoured direction, say twenty metres. New roots established themselves under the new trunks while the old ones died off. You'd be a long time walking to Ireland from France that way, though.)

The trees that established themselves here after the Ice Age are only considered to be native because they were not brought here by humans. Birds, mammals and the wind apparently are more natural than humans. Of course, no matter what kind of seeds arrived here they could only become established if conditions here were right. So the seeds of the mountain ash, excreted by birds who had feasted on rowan berries further south, could grow here quite soon after the Ice Age on the exposed tundra grasslands, but coconuts and avocado seeds swept here on ocean currents hadn't a snowball's chance in hell. In fact, they still arrive here and are noted in coastal high-tide detritus surveys, but we wait in vain for coconut-fringed islands with glorious sandy beaches. We do indeed have such beaches, but they are much more likely to be coveted by golf-course developers than greengrocers looking for supplies for the Hallowe'en market.

It is interesting to note that most of our smaller trees have either wind-blown seeds or berries. Thus forests of birch and willow could be set up as soon as there was enough soil and warmth to support the wind-blown seeds. The adventurous short-taken birds could rest in their branches and leave behind calling cards full of haws, sloes, holly, rowan, elderberries, cherries and seeds of the berries of spindle, guelder-rose, crab apple, juniper, whitebeam and yew. These all fell on fertile ground and their trees bore fruit encouraging the birds to stay. However, while the seeds in a juicy berry need to pass through the ins and outs of a bird's digestive system, the same cannot be said of nuts. Did anyone ever see an oak tree grow from a jay's dropping? Once a nut is eaten that's that, end of story.

So how did the oak, the hazel, the Scots pine and the alder get here, then? And, indeed, how clever is it of trees to put all their hopes for the next generation in tasty attractive seeds? Well, this is where the mammals came in. Ireland was still attached to Britain and France when red squirrels came whisking across with hazelnuts and pine seeds in their dear little paws. They thoughtfully buried these in the ground so that they would have supplies in the cold winter days ahead and then thoughtlessly forgot where they had stored them when the time came to eat them. Or maybe the winter itself was harsher than Squirrel Nutkin had bargained for and he never lived to dig up his store. But red squirrels don't eat acorns – far too many tannins for their delicate tummies – only their brasher cousins the grey squirrels, in the yet-to-be-discovered America, could eat these, and they themselves would only arrive here nine thousand years later, unnaturally brought here by humans. It is much more likely that oak trees arrived here as acorns in the bills of jays and rooks, who are rather partial to them to this day, and who like to bury the odd few to have a tasty treat when times get hard. Obviously, their memories are not a hundred per cent either, and the oaks that germinated from those forgotten acorns found the country very much to their liking. They quickly rose above all the others and only had to share their canopy status with the wind-transported ash and elm, which had been following hard on their heels. The sycamore, which also has wind-transported seeds and which does very well here today, started off from much further south in Europe and no easterly gale gusts could blow its seeds all the way from France across the sea, which surrounded Ireland by the time it had moseyed north that far. The nuts of the beech tree did make it to Britain without human intervention, but their mammal porters found the Irish Sea barring further progress, and beech had to wait for the Normans before adding Ireland to their list of 'countries we have visited'.

What about the arbutus, the strawberry tree? It has a decidedly odd distribution here. It is native in Cork and Kerry, so well known, in fact, that it is included in the place names: *caithne* is its name in Irish and Smerick in Kerry is called *Árd na Caithne* – the Height of the Arbutus. It is also native to Sligo, and nowhere in between. It is called the strawberry tree because it has a soft red fruit like a little strawberry. However, the resemblance ends there, as the fruit is not juicy and tasty to eat. It is edible – but you must wait until November, when it is really ripe, or otherwise you'll understand why it is called *Arbutus unedo* in Latin. According to Pliny, it is because a person will only eat one – *un edo*. However, as it is quite common in the Mediterranean regions, they make fruit tarts out of it, and in Corsica it is also eaten. They turn it into *gelée d'arbouses* there, according to Jane Grigson in her seminal *Fruit Book*. I must say I wasn't mad about the one I ate, nicked from a tree in a front garden in Rathmines in late November. It is no wonder that it only made the third division when the trees were being given importance in the old days. Useful trees like the oak, hazel, holly, yew, ash, Scots pine and apple were considered to be the nobles of the wood, and woe betide anyone who even cut a branch off one they didn't own. The second group, called the commoners, comprised birch, elm, wild cherry, alder, willow, hawthorn and rowan. The arbutus was lumped in along with blackthorn, elder, juniper, spindle, whitebeam and aspen in the lower divisions of the wood. It is a much more beautiful tree than any of the others in its group. Perhaps it just didn't grow near to whoever was making the divisions, or perhaps they ate the fruits when they were unripe, when they are in the same category as the sloes of the blackthorn of the whitebeam, which are always mouth-puckeringly sour. Certainly there was no sugar around in those days to make the fruit more palatable.

Trees were valued in those far-off days by what good could be got from them. If they had more than one benefit, then they were higher in the pecking order than ones that had only one use. Oak trees had the best of timber and its acorns could be used as animal feed. But who would have thought that they would turn out to be expert timekeepers and would be able to pinpoint down to the very year when events happened *fadó, fadó*? Because oak was such a fine timber for construction and because it grew so commonly in Ireland, it was used for roads, ships, chariots, castles – all sorts of construction was carried out in oak. If these timbers have survived to the present day, it is possible to say when they lived and died by looking at the rings in the timber. Growth rings form in trees that grow on a stop-start basis. At our latitudes, trees don't grow in winter. When the heat of spring and summer comes, they lash into growth, but come the shorter days in late autumn and winter, they down tools again until the following year. It doesn't really matter whether they are deciduous, losing their leaves in winter, or evergreen, like the northern pine and spruce. If it is too cold they stop growing whether or which. And this record of the stop-start growth is recorded in the growth rings. Years that were great for growth gave rise to very wide rings. Bad years for trees gave them narrow rings. And all the trees of the same species in the same country followed the same pattern. All the oak trees in Ireland grew poorly in a bad year and well in a good year. So by looking at the rings of a tree just felled, you could make a pattern of the rings over the years the tree was alive – bad, good, good, middling, not so good, bad, bad and so on. Of course, these patterns can be measured much more scientifically than this and a master pattern can be drawn up – the science of dendrochronology.

As older and older trees were found, the standard pattern got longer and longer and moved further and further back. It is for all the world like a bar code, with the growth pattern for oak trees in Ireland chronicled for every year. The pattern now extends back thousands of years. So any ancient piece of oak that is now found has the order of its rings compared with the master pattern, and we know exactly when that oak tree lived. So the oak timbers found in roads under the bogs in the midlands can be dated to the exact year. The road, obviously, was built from dead timbers, trees probably felled for that very purpose. Bog oaks that grew in Ireland before the climate changed and became suitable for blanket bog can be dated accurately and tell us when they died, suffocated by the growing blanket bog. Ships washed up on beaches by storm tides may well be ancient Armada ships. The venerable oak timbers will tell us the dates.

Trees nowadays are valued just for growing at all. By growing, they take in carbon dioxide from the atmosphere, and as long as they stay as timber and are not burnt or do not rot, they will hold on to that carbon. So if we want to remove carbon from the air in order to row back on global warming, then the thing to do is grow plenty of trees and keep the timber intact. The faster the tree grows, the more carbon dioxide it takes in. So in a new list of Irish noble trees, the willow species might get promotion, as they are the fastest-growing of all our native trees. Bring back the sally gardens!

MOONEY GOES WILD

AFTER NINE YEARS on the air for half an hour a week, on a Sunday, the radio programme on which I work, *Mooney Goes Wild,* got promotion, as it were, in 2004, to an hour a week at the weekend primetime slot of 10 am to 11 am on Saturday morning. Now, this is actually a live programme, much to the surprise of some people. We are all out in RTÉ way in advance of the programme on Saturdays, making sure it all happens without a glitch, on the hour. At times, when I am asked if it is live, I am tempted to respond, 'Barely', knowing, as I do, that many of the listeners are hearing the programme in bed, enjoying the Saturday-morning lie-ins they have that we don't.

The public are invited to phone in with comments and

queries, and it soon became apparent that there was a different class of listener on Saturday than we were used to from the Sunday programmes. First of all, they seemed to be touchier. An innocent remark by our bird expert on the advisability of feeding birds through the hard times – 'Keep up the social welfare,' said he – brought a very incensed response. Social welfare recipients were entitled to their payments – they weren't handouts – what did our panellist mean by such remarks?

But we weren't to be repressed by such reactions. We are normally not amused by listeners ringing up giving out about wildlife, but shortly after a particular outcry in the newspapers about urban-generated rural housing and the increase in people who work in the city coming to live in the country – a lifestyle considered to be unsustainable, depending as it does on heavy use of private transport – we got the following call. The house-owner wanted to know how to get rid of the fox that walked across his manicured lawn in the country and, on occasion, even had the temerity to leave a calling card. Well, I pulled no punches. I said that living in the country was wasted upon such a person and that he should take himself back to the city from whence he came. Such impertinence, to seek to get rid of a creature that had always lived there, just because he wanted to impose his unnatural lawn on the surroundings! I was gratified to receive a plethora of calls saying, Right on – I did my business right. No dissenting calls at all, or maybe they just didn't get through.

Mind you, I am amazed that we get any calls at all while we are on the air. Surely if you are listening to such a fascinating programme, you'd be reluctant to get up and phone, in case you missed pearls of wisdom while waiting to get through. And the latest now is emailing while the programme is on. It may be easier to type and listen, but it sure isn't possible for us to broadcast and read our emails at the same time. We are not coming down with extra assistants on a Saturday morning, and the people we do have are more than fully occupied with the phone lines.

Calls, I suppose, can be divided up into several categories. There are always the 'How do you get rid of...' calls. These start in April with 'How do you get rid of ants?' and I feel you could broadcast the same response, even the same programme, for a month, as people don't seem to listen to what you say and ask about getting rid of ants every week. This moves on to how to get rid of starlings and other bird species that have unwanted nests on our personal and private property. In 2004, there seems to have been an unmerciful invasion of millipedes in certain areas. These are black worm-like creatures with allegedly thousands of legs that feed on dead and rotting vegetation. One man encountered them in his bath, and wanted to know if they came up the plughole or through the overflow outlet. A bit of experimental activity would have resolved the mystery of how they got in: put the plug into the plughole. Surely they are not so super-strong that they could lift that. If they still appear, put Sellotape over the overflow outlet. Are they stuck to the inside of the Sellotape?

If you have an infestation, as people will insist on putting it, you must be providing food for them. Animals and insects are not on a fasting pilgrimage as they crawl all over your house. When did you last clean out the gutters and shores of dead leaves? Are there old birds' nests in your eaves? How can I tell, up in Donnybrook, what the cut of your premises is? But one thing is sure, if you have an infestation of millipedes or ants or flour mites in the press or silverfish in the kitchen at night, whatever, you are, however inadvertently and unwillingly, providing them with a source of food. Elementary, my dear Watson. Find the food supply and get rid of it and you'll be free of the unwanted visitor. But of course sometimes this is easier said than done. Anyway, millipedes do no harm at all. They think they look lovely, even if you don't. Sweep them back out of doors where they belong.

Another category of caller wants to report unusual wildlife occurrences. These are great and are seized upon with great alacrity, as they can often make great radio. We had the blackbird couple in Limerick who reared a chick in a nest which they had built in the Christmas tree in the hospital grounds in the month of January. Obviously the light and the heat of the bulbs fooled the birds into thinking it was spring. We ran the story until the baby blackbird was successfully fledged and out of the nest. We have calls about squirrels and rats at bird tables, robins that come when they are called, and ones which carry out duets with householders out at the clothes line, wrens that nest in tracksuit tops on the clothes line, slugs that bungee jump out of trees, foxes that saunter around houses – inside, that is – and cuckoos heard in February. We are expected to provide an explanation for all these phenomena, even though they may be sprung on us live on air. Like children clutching comfort blankets, we go in each week armed with a veritable library of books on every wildlife topic imaginable, but of course on the air there is never time to consult any of these learned tomes.

Another category of listener delights in ringing us up to give us more information on a topic we may have discussed on air, or rarely – very rarely – to inform us that we are wrong. Often, the latter come in the form of emails to the programme, and indeed emails are a great medium of communication between ourselves and the listeners. Pictures can be attached to emails and in some cases a picture can be worth a thousand words. The woman with the hummingbird in her back garden sent in a picture of the hummingbird hawk moth. We get wonderful close-ups, sometimes, of spiders and webs. Butterflies are easily identified from pictures too. We get great pictures of bungee-mating slugs.

We also have a category of listeners who seem to dislike wildlife and consider it as the enemy. We got a cross email from a lady on a beautiful May day giving out about all the dandelions that are around. Such cheerful, happy flowers!

She wasn't giving out about buttercups or primroses or bluebells or daisies. No, she seemed to be expressing some form of flower apartheid. Of course, the growing point of dandelions is down in the bottom of the flower, so mowing the blessed lawn only encourages them. Give up having a lawn – plant a tree instead and put a woodland wildflower garden in underneath. Dandelions don't grow in woods.

And what about the attitude of the sender of this email?

Would like to ask you a question. Grey crows and magpies are scavengers, they devour any animals that are killed on our roads, even rats, which we consider dirty animals. At present any amount of badgers are lying dead on the roads and remain there for many days without being touched. Why don't the crows and magpies eat badgers? Are farmers right that they are dirty, disease-carrying animals that nature itself won't even touch?

Such naked aggression and hatred for poor old *broc*! Of course, it is not true. We do see more dead badgers on the roads than other species that are lighter and swifter of foot. These lighter corpses are probably hurled into the hedges by our speeding motorcars as we thunder along at speeds in excess of what is safe, no matter what the speed limit says, particularly on smaller secondary roads. And is there a badger removal service? Not to my knowledge, so some natural scavenging process must be getting rid of them or we'd have wall-to-wall dead badger on the roads, such is their abundance in the first place and propensity to car slaughter in the second.

But it is the public response that makes the programme, and keeps it fresh and relevant. It keeps us on our toes, too, because, no matter how carefully the running order is planned in advance, the programme has a life of its own when it goes on air. We should make a programme some time consisting of the stuff we prepared earlier but never got time to broadcast on the day. But who's complaining when there is such public interest in the whole subject?

CHAPTER TWENTY ONE

THE **STATE** OF OUR **ENVIRONMENT**

IN MAY 2004, ten new countries joined the European Union. A great deal of work had gone on beforehand to make sure that these accession countries were up to the standards of the EU and were 'fit' to join. The main areas where they had to reach our standards were in environmental matters, and in standards of health and safety in the workplace. It certainly was a far cry from thirty years ago, when we joined. We all voted in favour, we were willing and anxious to behave like good Europeans and, above everything else, we were dying to benefit from the structural funds and the money from the Common Agricultural Policy that Europe had to offer. But it very soon became apparent that we only wanted to benefit, not to put ourselves out. We were, of course, bound by EU legislation, but one of the first things our politicians negotiated was a derogation from the waste directives. We were so far back and unready that we could not possibly comply, and so a fifteen-year derogation was acquired. As a result, we had no waste or waste problems in Ireland until 1987! Well, we didn't have to measure how much waste we had, there were no standards for landfill sites – aptly known then as dumps – recyling was unheard of. New member states today are allowed no derogations of any description; they can only join when they are up to the mark.

But we did things our way. There were air-quality regulations too. There were limits beyond which our air could not deteriorate without breaking these regulations and incurring the wrath of Europe. We must measure our air quality every day. Which we did, but of course we never published the measurements until the April following the winter when the worst air quality occurred. So you knew in April what had killed you last November! Or at least you could find out then when the air quality in urban areas exceeded the EU limits. In fact, it was only after the terrible first week in January 1982, when a yellow pall of smog hung over Dublin for five days, that the public began to demand to know what the air quality was now, not in three month's time. The authorities were forced to release daily figures, public awareness grew and the subsequent ban on the sale of smoky coal in urban areas from 1990 on was accepted.

But it was in the area of water quality that we really showed our ignorance and apathy. Sure, haven't we loads of water, isn't it always raining, what's the problem? Where to begin to explain? To put it simply, we take in clean water for our various uses and we put out dirty water when we are finished. God sends us new clean supplies of rain, and aren't we grand? goes the thinking. But the Environment Protection Agency (EPA) measures our water quality and they are not so sanguine about it.

Let's take drinking water first. It is vital for a country to have plentiful supplies of clean, fresh, disease-free water. Our drinking water can come from surface supplies, such as lakes and rivers, or from the groundwater, which really means artificial wells. Most of us get our water from surface waters, pumped to our homes by public water schemes, for which we don't pay, and indeed many of us have no intention of ever paying for it. The public water-supply schemes ensure that the water they send out is free from any sort of contamination and, according to the latest EPA report (2003), they got it right 97.4 per cent of the time. However, we are not all on public water schemes. There are over five and a half thousand 'group' (privately run) water schemes in Ireland, many of which get their water from groundwater. Last year's EPA report showed that 26 per cent – more than a quarter – of them were contaminated with coliform bacteria, which only come from the intestines of humans or animals. In other words, more than a thousand private water schemes in Ireland are contaminated with sewage and slurry. Charming!

Where does this pollution come from and how does it get into our water supplies? Human waste is sewage, and this can't be discharged willy-nilly into the environment – or can it? The good old EPA have the story. There is, of course, an EU urban waste water treatment directive, which we transposed into Irish law in 1994. The government target for full compliance, you'll be glad to know, is 2005. At that time, in 1994, 48 per cent of our urban sewage was discharged into our waters completely untreated, and another 35 per cent only received primary treatment, which just meant the big solid lumps were sieved out or settled under gravity, but the dirty water happily flowed into our seas, lakes and rivers. In case you can't bear to do the sums, I will – that was a massive 83 per cent of all our urban sewage. We got EU cohesion funds and fixed up the situation, however. Ringsend was upgraded, which meant that Dublin's waste water is now treated, since May 2003, and we are therefore 69 per cent compliant with the EU waste water directive. Another 31 per cent to go before the end of 2005. There won't be any more cohesion funds, though – sure, hasn't Ireland's financial situation improved and aren't our new members much more needy? We don't begrudge them; we got more than our share of it in our time. We'll pay to improve our waste-water treatment from our own taxes – isn't that what they're for?

Of course, there's more to it than urban waste-water treatment plants. What happens if you want to live in an area not serviced by 'mains'. No problem – you build your very own septic tank on the half-acre and that takes care of everything. It does, if you do it right, if you desludge your tank frequently and refrain from killing, with bleaches and other horrible unnecessary toilet cleaners, the bacteria that are breaking down your organic waste in the properly sized percolation area. Otherwise, where do you think the stuff goes when you pull the chain? It ends up, unbroken-down, in the groundwater, in your neighbour's well, in the group water scheme, in the local river, in some cases in your own well if you really haven't taken care. There are group waste-water schemes, where the waste of up to a hundred individuals can be sustainably treated in an environment-friendly reedbed system. We actually have some such schemes in Ireland, but not many. We don't want to live near enough to anyone to share a waste-water scheme of any description. Forty-three per cent of all the new houses built in 2002 were one-off housing built in increasingly remote areas, because of the attraction of scenic isolation and cheap land. No mains sewage disposal then, or indeed public clean water supplies either. Take out some shares in one of the bottled water companies while you are at it!

But doesn't it rain great quantities of clean water down on top of us every season? It does, and we could use that water as it comes, if we caught it on our roofs and piped it into our homes to wash clothes, flush toilets and so on. It would save us having to use expensively cleaned fit-to-drink water for these things, but what the hell, sure we are not paying for the expensively cleaned water. Anyway, if it was that important, wouldn't there be building regulations making new houses built on half-acres with plenty of space have a rainwater collection system of downpipes and gutters and a dual water plumbing system? I used to live in such a house, which was built in the 1950s, but of course we are much more advanced now. All the rainwater that falls on our roofs nowadays is piped straight into the storm-water sewers and causes huge problems of waste-water volume at the treatment works during very wet periods. Or at least it would if there weren't overflow valves that could be opened, discharging the whole lot, rain and waste water together, into the nearest river. There is no time to hold it for treatment when there is such a volume coming through. Remember, we had no environmental studies taught in any of our schools between 1936 and 1971, so how could those in charge possibly know these things and how can we, the public, know either, to demand proper treatment of water and sewage? This excuse should be good for another ten years yet!

So the uncaught rain falls down onto the ground, and if the ground is not covered in tarmac or concrete (in which case the rainwater ends up in the storm-water overflows), it percolates down through the soil to replenish the groundwater supplies. Or it flows, with gravity, through the soil into the rivers and lakes. It's very good at dissolving things along the way, so what does the clean rainwater find in our soils? Do you really want to know? Could you bear it? Well, it finds all the things we put there to get rid of. Chief among these are animal slurries. In the bad old pre-EU days, our cattle lived out in the fields, ate the grass, grew slowly, put up with the winter and did their droppings as they went along, a cow pat here, another there. They were fairly healthy too, in the main – OK, maybe they had the odd dose of worms or scour, but they got over it. And the dung beetles broke down the well-distributed cowpats, and the bacteria helped, and there was nothing nasty left to be dissolved and washed down by the rain. But farmers weren't rich. In the 1970s, when we first joined Europe, we had a market on our doorstep that would pay good money for every bit of beef and every drop of milk we produced. Keeping cattle indoors in the bad weather increased production. We got grants to build slatted sheds, we got grants to 'improve' marshy wet places that weren't worth farming before and to remove hedges to make bigger fields, we got grants to arterially drain rivers in order to have more farmland, we could reseed our pastures with one or two species of grass instead of having to put up with whatever grew there naturally, we could add nitrates and phosphates to make the grass grow better, we could give our animals medicines to prevent the possibility that they might get sick, and no matter how much we produced there was always intervention to store beef and butter mountains and milk lakes – we got top price. We could spread the slurries, saved during the winter in the slurry pits, over the soil to increase the supplies of nitrates and phosphates. We could cut silage two or three times a year instead of having to risk the weather and save the hay. It was great.

It was, until the plain citizen of Europe realised how much of the whole EU budget was going on agriculture and called for CAP reform. Quotas were introduced. Grants were given for things that were needed, rather than things that were not. On a European scale, sheep were needed, so we all turned to rearing sheep. The ewe premium was introduced in 1980, and by 1992 the national flock had grown by 270 per cent. We had nine million sheep in Ireland in the early 1990s and, as a result, 20 per cent of our uplands are affected by soil erosion. More CAP reform followed, this time in the form of grants to farm wisely and REPS – the Rural Environment Protection Scheme – was introduced. The EU nitrates directive was issued in 1991 too, obliging all member states to take action to reduce pollution from too much nitrate, but sure what were we to do with our slurries? We ignored the directive as long as we could and only began to talk about implementing it very reluctantly in 2004.

Does it matter? What is the state of the place now – particularly our water bodies? The EPA monitors away and produces reports regularly. The latest report, issued in 2004, makes depressing reading. To put it simply, our water quality is declining. More than one-third of the river-monitoring stations – 38 per cent – are not compliant with the regulations, which is EPA-speak for the fact that 4800 kilometres of river channel has some degree of pollution. Our lakes are equally bad. There is information collected for two hundred and thirty-eight lakes, and of these, eighty-six – or 36 per cent – are polluted. Cavan, Monaghan and Leitrim are at the top of the table for polluted lakes. Fifty per cent of the springs and wells in the Burren are contaminated, particularly after rain.

What are we doing to our country and do we care? Well, no, it would seem. We have a God-given right to do what we like – to build wherever we like, but have piped water and flush toilets, to improve our land and farm intensively, to plant forests of Sitka spruce, regardless of whether they acidify or not. Anyone that has the temerity to point out the irreversible harm this is doing to our environment is shouted down or accused of being a snob. Proper, good county development plans are overturned by private councillors' motions to favour party voters. Attempts to make the polluter pay are outwitted by illegal dumping, littering and refusal to pay bin charges. Our ten new member states greatly enlarge our European total of unpolluted water and pristine wildlife habitats. How long will it remain so? If their attitude to EU membership is anything like ours was, I don't give it very long.

CHAPTER TWENTY TWO

TEACHING STUDENTS –
OR **NOT** TEACHING THEM

TEACHING CAN BE WONDERFUL. I should know. I come from a line of teachers on both sides, and I do a bit of teaching myself. Not that I *am* a teacher mind you. Full time, all day, every day, it must be one of the most demanding occupations ever. You are totally committed when you stand up in front of that class. You have to initiate proceedings, keep the show going. If your attention flags or you show boredom even for a minute, the whole thing collapses. Because the truth is that, in the main, pupils don't want to be taught. They might like being at school, all right, but they'd rather occupy themselves in any other way in class than in listening to a lesson. The feedback is instant. If the lesson is not hitting the spot, they are bored and they show it. It is very hard to hit the spot for five hours a day with a class of up to thirty individuals of varying motivation and interest. In an office job you could have a break, a cup of coffee or take a phone-call – not in class, you can't. Teachers deserve a high spot in heaven.

My teaching experiences are different, because I come into the classroom as a one-off – a novelty, someone who was invited. The teacher is present. The pupils are allegedly on their best behaviour. I may be talking to primary or post-primary pupils, and my only requirement is to be interesting enough to hold the attention of the pupils. If not, the reaction is swift and merciless. Unlike grown-up audiences, which, if bored, merely switch off and look out the window, pupils who are not enjoying their lessons make it known. They lean back on their chairs and indeed fall off them, which livens up proceedings considerably. They plait the hair of the girl in front of them. They reflect the sunlight on to your face with the front of their watches. They speak to each other – what they have to say is considerably more relevant than what they have to listen to – and, if they are a particularly obnoxious group, they join together to mock the accent of the speaker and find double meanings in everything that is said. But at least I never have to mark copies or correct exam papers at primary or secondary level, so I can continue with the self-delusion that if it was all right on the day, then what I said made an indelible impression and they have really understood and learnt.

My third-level teaching experiences are somewhat different. Here I am actually not a teacher but a lecturer, and that title somehow implies that the task merely means passing on information to rapt, enthusiastic young adults who have actually chosen further education after their Leaving Cert, and have specifically selected the area in which you lecture. Yes, well, maybe so, but the be-riveting-and-keep-my-attention rule applies here too. So you are, and you do, and you get through a whole year on the topic with a class still turning up at the end of the year and even the occasional one asking relevant questions.

And then come the exams. You have to set a paper on the subject you have taught and, under time pressure, in three hours, they return what I can only assume is their best attempt to pass, based on what they have learnt from you over the year. Could this be all they really know about the subject, after all your hard work and Oscar-winning lecturing performances? It's depressing.

I lecture in biogeography in a third-level establishment. This is a subject that covers what plants and animals live where in the world and why. Why are there kangaroos in Australia, llamas in South America and deer in Europe – all grass-eating herbivores, yet so different? The subject involves descriptions of conditions in rainforests and in deserts and explanations for what species we have or don't have in Ireland. So the exam questions reflect what I have covered. One year, I asked the pupils to describe deserts and the plants and animals that lived there. (Despite having written the word on the exam paper in the question, I got long accounts of *desserts* rather than deserts.) Plants and animals in deserts have to cope with great heat and a lack of water. Could my pupils perhaps tell me about some of these?

Well, you will be delighted to know that camels are really well adapted to desert life. One student told me that they can lose 400 per cent of their body weight through dehydration before any permanent damage happens to them. I tried to imagine such a camel. Another said that a camel can lose 25 per cent of its body weight before it becomes dangerous.

Some animals in deserts have extremely large ears. This part is actually true: it's so that they can dissipate heat through such a large surface area and survive. We use the same phenomenon to heat our houses. We have things with a large surface area giving off heat in our rooms. We call these radiators. They are filled with hot water and they lose heat rapidly through the surfaces and warm our rooms. (Got that?) Well, sensibly enough, the ears on the desert animals are also called radiator ears, because that's how they function too, and foxes, hares and hedgehogs in deserts in different parts of the world have them in order to survive. That's not how my students understand it, though. They tell me that radiator ears contract and expand during hot daily temperatures – a case of now you see them, now you don't, I suppose. They tell me that the animals can store water in their ears because they are radiators. They say that they reflect the sun – like car mirrors I suppose.

Their knowledge of desert plants is not much better. Plants in deserts grow downwards instead of upwards, they tell me. The creosote plant sends out seeds via its roots. Cacti are spineless. Desert plants excrete salt, but this often clogs up the sellers (*sic*). Some plants have adapted to desert conditions by having smaller leaves, while others survive *by disappearing altogether*. How could they think I told them that?

Some years, the exam question might be about rainforests – describe them and talk about the threats to them. Did you know that the rainforest has a fourteen-month year, and that the trees there take millions of years to grow? I didn't. The trees there have no seeds and will soon be distinct (*sic*). Rubber trees were very popular once and were cut down and used before plastic was invented, according to a student of mine; and another one told me that the rubber tree has often been cut down. (I suppose it must spring back again after each cutting so that it can be re-cut.) There is a teak-flavoured mahogany tree there, apparently. One plant called Bunka banks (whatever that might be) is a 'scented angiosperm' that drinks the sap of other trees. (Actually, most plants are angiosperms; it simply means that they have flowers and fruit.) The sun shines twenty-four hours a day there. Many of the animals are 'docturnal'. And on threats to the rainforest – once a tree is cut down, it won't grow. Well, well. When trees are cut down, the climate usually sores (*sic*). There is an increase in ground-freezing birds, whatever they are.

Their knowledge of Irish wildlife is not so hectic either. Another type of vegetation found in Ireland is the flora and fauna, according to my students. The trees in Ireland are very young – they are only 10,000 years old. Hedgerows are boarders (*sic*) for fields. Corncrakes have become scarce here because they are too long for the Sahara desert! When forest clearances occurred in Ireland, the eagles began to eat the grass and the small baby animals. Soils in Ireland exist in three states – solid, liquid and gas. Many soils in Ireland are broken into smaller soils. Many species became extinct when our forests were cut down, but some were able to stick threw (*sic*) it.

It's terrible reading this. What impression have they gone away with? What will they tell the young people of Ireland when they go out to teach themselves? But at least I haven't had to read what was written for one of my colleagues. He was lecturing about habitations – why cities are where they are, on trade routes, at river mouths and so on. But nowadays, he explained to his class, cities can actually be imposed on places that have no natural attraction for them. Some cities in the American desert have been entirely artificially created. All food and water is brought in by road and processed there. Why, they even have their own Coca Cola plant. This came back on the exam script as follows: it is possible nowadays to have a city anywhere; they have such a city in America where everything is supplied and the Coca Cola grows on trees.

HAVING A **WHALE** OF A TIME

WHEN HUMANS DISCOVERED how to use and control fire, civilisation could make two enormous leaps. The first was that now food could be cooked as required, instead of taking advantage of a lightning-caused forest fire or, as Charles Lamb would have it (according to an essay of his that used to be on the old Inter Cert syllabus), waiting for a house to burn down with a pig inside it before enjoying roast pork – a likely story. The second great leap that being able to control fire allowed was the possibility of seeing in the dark. Burning brands of wood could light up places that were never exposed to daylight. Very early cave drawings were done in dark places, far from daylight, which indicates that the artists were part of a community that could use fire to provide artificial light.

Burning brands, however, didn't last very long. Who was it, I wonder, who discovered that oils and fats with a wick in the centre would make a light that was somewhat safer and would last much longer? Animal fats and beeswax were obvious sources for such candle material, and plants such as rushes could act as wicks. Animal fat, or tallow, gave smoky, smelly light and beeswax was a scarce enough commodity. But there was another source of oil – animals that lived in the seas had great quantities of oil, in the form of blubber, in their bodies, and it was discovered that this too could be used for light. Seals could be caught reasonably easily, as they had to haul out on to the land to give birth, and so were vulnerable to capture at this time. For millennia, seals have been hunted for oil for lamps.

There were other animals in the sea that also had stores of oil and, as man became proficient in making boats, these animals could be hunted. The Greenland shark was hunted by the Inuit and by Icelanders for its oil-filled liver. Sharks as a group have no swim bladder and, in the absence of such a piece of equipment, the oil-filled liver adds to their buoyancy and helps to prevent them from sinking. It is not as good as a swim bladder, however, and sharks have to swim continuously to stay afloat. The Greenland shark is a slow, lumbering creature that can be caught from small boats, but sharks in general never really featured as a major source of world oil – I wouldn't fancy asking a great white shark for a liver transplant, would you?

But bigger and better than any shark or seal, whales were the business when you were really serious about collecting oil. Once man had boats big enough, the whales, which of course never came ashore, could be hunted and killed for their oil. The earliest whalers used stone axes to kill whales, and there are records of whales being taken as far back as the Book of Isaiah, in the Old Testament, when it is the Lord who is being accused of punishing the Leviathan with his strong sword. We also have the biblical story of Jonah and the whale, but Jonah wasn't out whaling – he just got chucked overboard when his shipmates decided that he and his sins were the source of their troubles and cause of a huge storm they got caught in. Instantly, the sea was calm, but poor Jonah was swallowed by a whale with yawning jaws and ivory teeth. At least it wasn't a baleen whale, or he would never have got past the baleen filter. As it was, he passed straight through, unscathed, into the whale's stomach, where the digestive juices were put on hold, for some reason, allowing Jonah to be duly expelled, still unscathed, three days later, up from the whale's lower regions, back through his mouth on to dry land in the region of Nineveh, a city on the river Tigris. A Turkish mosque was built in Nineveh in honour of Jonah and, true to his means of transport, there was a miraculous lamp there which burnt perpetually without any oil at all.

Whaling, which is catching whales for oil and food, goes

back to the Stone Age, when Inuit people caught whales from skin boats using stone harpoons and lines made of skin. Natives of northern Japan used to catch whales too. They struck them with poisoned spearheads and waited for them to die and float to the surface. The Norse certainly had a whaling industry going from the end of the ninth century. King Alfred of England writes, in AD 890, of a visitor to England who had come with a view to catching whales there. This visitor, one Octher, was proficient at catching whales in his own country – wherever that was; Alfred doesn't say.

However, it was the Basques who really got whaling going from the eleventh century onwards. They hunted the North Atlantic whale for five centuries in the Bay of Biscay. This was a manageable whale to hunt from small boats. It lived in shallow inshore waters, mostly within twenty miles of the coast, it swam slowly and, most important of all, it floated when it was dead. So it was known as the Atlantic 'right' whale. It provided lots of oil from its blubber – up to about twenty tonnes – and from its large tongue and lower lip. It also provided a commodity called whalebone. This was not what you might think – the skeleton of the whale – but great sheets of baleen, which hang from the roof of its mouth. The whale uses them for feeding. It draws in a great quantity of water through these big sheets, which act like a sieve. All the food in the water is filtered out by the baleen, and the water trickles back into the sea. The whale then licks the food off the baleen sheets with its tongue. This huge creature, which could reach up to fifty-five feet long and weigh over eighty tonnes, gets all its sustenance from the admittedly very large amounts of very small planktonic creatures which individually might be no more than three millimetres long.

This baleen or whalebone was of the utmost use in the days before plastic. It was much in demand for the manufacture of stays and corsets, those most restrictive of undergarments that no respectable woman would venture out without. Whalebone was flexible and long lasting and ladies' fashions from the Elizabethan age onwards demanded great quantities.

Whale-meat did not keep well, so it could only be eaten if the boat returned home pretty smartly with the carcass. Hunting the Atlantic right whale had been going on off the European coast for five hundred years when, at the end of the sixteenth century, great efforts were being made by European explorers to find the northwest passage. As they tried for years in the cold Arctic waters, they found something more immediately valuable – the Greenland right whale, known today as the bowhead. This whale has even more enormous quantities of baleen in its mouth. Each plate can be fifteen feet long and it has up to three hundred and forty plates on each side of its mouth. That sure was a lot of corsets and umbrella spokes! They hunted this enormous whale almost to extinction in less than a hundred years. It is still extremely rare and is totally protected today.

Even though there were now bigger sailing ships that

could go further afield and hunt whales across the Atlantic, not just off shore, the blubber still had to be brought home and processed fairly sharpish. So it was considered a great advance when they could equip the whaling ships with the means to melt down the blubber at sea. This involved building a brick oven on the ship, where a fire could be lit and the blubber melted and stored in barrels in the hold. These try works, as they were called, were invented in the 1760s and meant that whaling ships could stay at sea for longer periods and hunt and kill many whales. Which was terrible really, as by this stage the stocks of right whales in the Atlantic were greatly diminished. Now with the try works on board, American whaling ships from Newfoundland could set off on journeys lasting up to four years and come back with their ships laden down with oil. They could sail around the Cape of Good Hope and Cape Horn and hunt in all the oceans of the world. And they discovered a southern right whale as well, which lived south of the equator. But they also discovered that they could catch an even more valuable whale – the sperm whale, which lived in the deepest waters, between forty degrees north and forty degrees south, and could not be caught by small boats from land. This whale has seasonal wanderings to polar latitudes and occurred in Atlantic waters at certain times of the year.

This whale is a toothed whale, not a baleen one, and it feeds on squid and octopus, including the almost unknown giant squid, which it catches at depths of 3000 metres. Its ability to dive to these great depths and stay there for up to an hour at a time is facilitated by the fact that its huge head, which is a third the size of its body, is filled with a waxy substance called spermaceti. Deep down in the ocean, this cools and hardens, allowing the whale to stay down there. Upon rising, the whale can pump warm blood around it and so melt it and increase its own buoyancy, allowing it to float. This spermaceti was the treasure that the sperm whalers sought. It was the purest and most magnificent of oils. It made marvellous candles. In fact, a measure of light in the old standards – the candle power unit of illumination – was based on the illuminating power of candles made from this oil. The world depended on whale oil for light in the 1700s, and for half the 1800s too, and the sperm whale was the prized donor.

Herman Melville gives a first-hand account of sperm whaling in *Moby Dick*, written in 1850. It certainly wasn't a job for the faint-hearted. The big whaling ship, under full sail, got into waters where the whales were. The lookout from the masthead spotted the whale blowing as it came up for air. The ship sailed as near as possible and then the whalers left the ship in quickly launched, keel-less boats like *currachs*, and rowed after the whale. When they got near enough, the harpooner stood up in the front of the boat and threw a steel harpoon at the head of the whale. This had a long rope attached to it, the other end of which was held by the men in the boat. They wore the enormous creature out, and threw more harpoons into it as they chased it.

Dangerous work. The whale could and sometimes did beach the boat with its enormous flukes at the tail, or by coming up under the boat. The water all round seethed with sharks lured by the smell of blood from the whale. Woe betide any sailor that fell out of the boat! The rope attached to the first harpoon moved at such speed, as it was paid out, that it could remove a limb from an unwary sailor. But worse than all of this, the whale met a terrible end. The hunters harpooned it till blood came up through its blow hole. Even if it dived and escaped, it still had the harpoon embedded in it, which would cause a slow, lingering death later.

Sperm whales have a very large brain relative to the size of their body. Whales share with elephants the distinction of having, relative to the size of their bodies, bigger brains than man. If size equals space to learn and remember, then it is no wonder that elephants and Moby Dick never forget.

Sperm whales were also hunted on their journeys across the Atlantic, going to and from their tropical breeding grounds. They would feed off the continental shelf in late summer and autumn and would sometimes come in to shallower, inshore waters, where they could be caught by European whalers in big sailing ships, before the invention of the try works, and brought ashore for processing.

An interesting substance was occasionally found in the intestines of the sperm whale. This was a waxy substance like soap, called ambergris or grey amber, though it has nothing to do with actual amber, which is fossilised resin.

This substance found in the sperm whale was beautifully perfumed and was in great demand by manufacturers of fine perfume as a fixative. Until relatively recently it was used by the some of the famous French perfume houses. Melville describes in great detail the collection of it from a dead, dehydrated sperm whale. He maintained that it only formed in the bowels of sick whales, that it was caused by indigestion and that they found hard parts of squid embedded in it. Whatever caused it, ambergris was certainly more precious than gold: the ship's mate was reckoning on a gold guinea an ounce from the druggists when he got back to land.

They were dangerous times. Whalemen often came back in a different ship to that in which they sailed, if they came back at all. But if they succeeded in landing four years' worth of sperm oil, their fortunes were made. As well as for light, the oil was also needed as a lubricant for machinery as the industrial age got going. But then mineral oil was discovered in America in 1859. Hydrocarbons could replace fatty lipids. Paraffin wax and oil could give light, and lubrication of all sorts could be provided by the mineral oil. There was no need to endanger life and limb any more, and what was left of the whale populations was saved, because right whales and sperm whales were no longer the only substantial source of oil. And indeed, for a very little while, the whaling industry declined. Fast-swimming whales such as blue whales and fin whales were impossible to catch from rowing boats, even ones launched from whaling ships at sea, and anyway their bodies sank when they were dead. So everything might have been OK for the whales, only that then, in 1864, a Norwegian named Svend Foyn invented a gun that could fire harpoons with an explosive head. These could be fired from the deck of the fast new steam-powered ships, and the fate of all whales was sealed. Everything was game now – not fair game, though, since no species of whale could now escape capture. These steamships, able to travel independently of the wind, could catch the species that up to then had remained unhunted.

Modern whaling began in the north Atlantic in 1870 and whaling stations were set up ashore to deal with the catches as they came back. We had such whaling stations in Ireland. Two Norwegian companies ran a whaling business in County Mayo, one on the south Iniskea Island from 1908 to 1914, and the other on the Mullet peninsula from 1909 until 1923 (interrupted for a few years in the middle because of the World War I). And, unbelievable as it might seem to many of us who believe that whales are creatures of faraway waters, eight hundred and ninety-nine whales were processed in those two stations during that time. They were mainly the faster-swimming whales, which could now be caught and killed with the new equipment – 592 fin whales, 125 blue whales, 97 sei whales – but sixty-three sperm whales and five humpback whales were processed here too, caught in the Atlantic no doubt. What did they want these whales for now? What excuse was there for hunting, practically to extinction, the Leviathans of our waters? We had another source of oil. Bustles were going out of fashion. Why continue to hunt and kill? Well, people still wanted the oil, and ashore in the stations they could extract oil not only from blubber, but from also from the skeletal bones in pressure-cooker-type extractors. This oil was used for linoleum, margarine, soap, crayons, lipstick and ice-cream as well as for lamps. The leftover bones were processed for bone meal. The flesh was canned and sent to countries, such as Japan, Norway and Iceland, that had a tradition of eating whale-meat since the days of local catches. Inedible flesh was sold as animal food. At their height, these whaling stations could process an entire hundred-tonne blue whale within thirty-six hours of its being killed. They quickly fished the Atlantic out, and the European whaling stations closed for lack of whales in the early 1920s.

But things got worse. Large factory whaling ships were built that could process an entire whale at sea. As well as try works, now known as blubber boilers, these were equipped with refrigeration plants, meat and bone-meal plants and, worst of all, sonar and other ultrasonic devices to frighten the whales into flight and exhaustion. Whale-meat was sold in Britain during World War II, when there was a shortage of other supplies of meat.

Modern fleets now rely on radar, depth recorders and underwater range finders to locate whales, because, incredible as it may seem, whales are still being hunted in some parts of the world. After World War II, in 1946 (when cows became plentiful again!), the International Whaling Commission was established with the aim of exploitation without extermination. Their role was to establish, for example, how many whales could be taken each year without decreasing the stocks. It quickly became apparent that this was closing the stable door after the horse had bolted. Many of our whales were practically extinct by now and could never be hunted again. Were they so scarce in world waters that they could never meet each other to mate and breed? This was for the IWC to decide. All taking of the Atlantic right whale and the grey whale was immediately banned, as was all taking of females of any whale species with calves. But other species could be hunted and so they declined too. By 1963, the numbers of blue whale had declined to less than a thousand worldwide, from an estimated 200,000 once upon a time, in the southern hemisphere alone. This whale was given total protection in 1966, by which time it wasn't worth anyone's while going hunting it anyway, and so the whalers moved on to the fin whale and the sei whale, which were not banned. Having been practically fished out worldwide by the 1970s (the Atlantic had already been cleaned out by the 1920s), the fin whale was put on the protected list in 1976. Today, only an aboriginal population in west Greenland are allowed to catch a very limited quota.

And so, on to the next one. The smaller sei whale was now worth chasing, as there were no longer any bigger whales that could be hunted. This whale first became almost extinct in the North Atlantic, and then the chase pursued it to the southern waters in the big factory ships, and at one point 20,000 were being taken annually. It too was finally put on the protected list when there were no more to catch profitably – in 1978 for the southern hemisphere; none have been caught in northern waters since 1988. Sperm whaling was only stopped in 1985, and humpbacks, which were practically extinct by that stage anyway in the north Atlantic, were protected there in 1956 and eventually worldwide (no quotas or exceptions) in 1988.

Not all countries of the world are members of the International Whaling Commission. These countries don't feel bound by its rulings and they seek quotas for research purposes. Iceland is one such country, which wishes to have a quota of minke whales to catch each year. We spoke to their minister for fisheries during our visit there in February 2004, and his attitude was illuminating to us, coming from Ireland, the waters of which are a whale and dolphin sanctuary since Charles Haughey brought in the legislation in 1991. The Icelandic fishing minister pointed out to us how important the fishing industry is to Iceland (which the British know only too well since the 'cod wars' of recent times). With the practical extinction of other whales, such as the blue whale and the fin whale, the minke whale seems to have recovered somewhat quicker, by exploiting the food sources that would have been eaten by these slower-to-recover species. Minke whales, although they are baleen whales, feed on fish, which they trap in their baleen sieves, rather than on plankton, which is the food of other baleen whales. The Icelandic fisheries minister maintained that 10 per cent of their fish catch of cod was being taken by minke whales, and they were determined to go back to catching them in order to protect their fish stocks. When we ventured to suggest that this would be very bad for their tourism industry and that surely inviting visitors to whale-watch was the way forward, he practically snorted. Ten per cent of the fishing industry was worth more to the economy of Iceland than the whole of their tourism industry, and anyway he was the minister for fisheries, not tourism. They had been taking some minke whales under licence each year up to this, to ascertain what they ate, how quickly they bred and where they fed, and he was sure they were a threat to the fishing industry. And, yes, the whale-meat is good to eat, and those whales captured under licence ended up in the meat shops when the research was finished.

I couldn't wait to go looking for whale-meat on sale. Was it in the butcher's, the fishmonger's, the supermarket? In the event, it wasn't anywhere, as it is only on sale in the summer time, when the whales are caught, not in February, when we were there. But it got me thinking: what was whale like to eat. I consulted my trusty Larousse Gastronomique, and there it was on page 1006. Whale meat was called *crapois* in the Middle Ages in France and was sold as 'Lenten bacon', for eating on the many meatless days they had then. It was a staple food of the poor. The Basque fishermen, who caught the right whale in the Atlantic for its oil, did a nice sideline in whale victuals. But what was it like to eat? Larousse pontificates: 'The flesh of this cetacean is most indigestible and remains tough even after twenty-four hours' cooking.' No pressure cookers around then, obviously. And what does it taste like? Larousse doesn't fail me here either: 'Boil a piece of lean beef in water which has been used to wash a not-too-fresh mackerel, and you will have a dish that is similar to escalope of whale *à la Valois*.' I haven't tried it yet. However, I wasn't too impressed by the final sentence in the entry in Larousse under 'whale', written, admittedly, in 1938. I quote it verbatim: 'Is it not certain, is it not an inescapable fact, that all animals living on land, swimming in water or flying in the air must sooner, or later, play their part in the culinary repertoire of the world?' The French approach to food neatly encapsulated, n'est-ce pas?

Another source of worry about whales in recent times is the frequency of beaching occurrences. Whales communicate by sound underwater. It is feared that man-made sounds from blasting and exploring, seismic shocks and sonic booms all interfere with the whales' perceptions of sounds. And there is the increasing pollution of our waters with heavy metals, which build up in the food chain, becoming most concentrated in those who, like whales, are at the top of the food chain. And there is the conflict between the top predators for the fish stocks – man and cetaceans. Who is entitled to them? Cetaceans also get caught inadvertently in fishing nets. And climate change is affecting our oceans and our ocean currents.

Whales first evolved in waters around Pakistan about 50 million years ago. The *Homo sapiens* species is here a mere 170,000 years. Doesn't this account of us and whales make us so proud of our species and its attitude to the rest of the inhabitants with which we share the world?

However, amazingly, whales are not extinct. Some species are recovering better than others and the fact that our waters have been a sanctuary for the last thirteen years has helped. There are fourteen different whale species on the Irish list at the moment, including the blue, sperm and humpback whales. It is possible to see them from our headlands if you are there at the right time with your binoculars. The Irish Whale and Dolphin Group studies the distribution and status of our whales and organises whale-watching expeditions, so at least some members of our species have a better attitude to whales.